FORGOTTEN

An innocent man left with permanent psychological injuries by the Metropolitan Police Force after reporting the abuse that had gone on for twenty years.

SHIKESH SORATHIA

Written by Shikesh Sorathia.
Edited by Shikesh Sorathia.
Published by Shikesh Sorathia.

The events that are described in this book are all true and to the best of Shikesh Sorathia's knowledge.

ISBN-13: 978-1-9164576-2-1

DEDICATION

I am dedicating this book to all victims, survivors, and allies that have been made to feel unheard and unseen by anyone in a position of power.

I hope that this book brings you some form of closure in your own way to help you in being able to live with the past while building and living a new life of your own choosing.

Life may turn out in a way we didn't want it to, but we are then guided to live it in the way we are meant to, and as we take a step back and admire the beauty of nature, we have the same reaction as Mr. Bean when he see's the sale on New Years Day - "Ooooh..."

Shikosh S

EPIGRAPH

"To keep your control over your truth and still have a voice, it may involve walking away from something or someone that may have tried to rewrite your truth while aiming to silence you for good."

- Shikesh Sorathia

CONTENTS

AUTHOR'S NOTE

I published my first book **ALMOST (ISBN-13: 978-1-9164576-0-7)** in November 2018 and until July 2024, several events had taken place in my life both personal and professional. This helped me to understand that a second and final book had to be written.

Unlike **ALMOST,** this book doesn't have any dialogue, as it's more about sharing the events that unfolded after I had finally escaped in October 2018 because of a life-or-death scenario.

In this book, I have referred to the abusers as 'male parent, female parent, eldest male sibling and younger male sibling' because referring to them as what they once may have portrayed no longer sits well with me from the ways they have left me feeling.

By writing this book, I am concluding my entire journey of living through several years of abuse and then facing the aftermath.

PLEASE BE AWARE:

The links to my social media accounts that were mentioned in **ALMOST** on the **About The Author** page when I had first published it, they are no longer working as I stopped using those accounts, so I have updated that page in **ALMOST**.

Also, the link to my life coaching website that was mentioned on the same page has been taken over by someone else who isn't known to me, so please don't trust that link because it's a fake account using my name. Even though they have stopped using it now, they could start using it again.

I had reported it all to the police as they were posting blog posts about subjects that I have never been involved in.

Thank you.

ACKNOWLEDGMENTS

I want to thank my inner child that has always kept my fighting spirit alive, so this one is for the seven-year-old Shikesh who set out to know the truth and even though he didn't know what he would have to face until he was thirty-two years of age, nothing was able to stop him from speaking his truth and exposing the abuse.

I also want to thank every single person that has played a role in helping me to get to this stage in my life today. Without all of you, my achievements to date wouldn't have been possible, so from the bottom of my heart, thank you!

Chapter One

The Escape

It was around July or August 2018 when the male parent had begun home improvements. I assumed that he just wanted to brighten up the house, but soon after, I had seen the 'For Sale' sign displayed in front of the house.

Have you ever experienced something where it felt like your heart stopped and you were desperate to catch a breath? That's what I felt in that moment because I began to panic and didn't know how to stop that feeling from taking over my entire mind and body.

I was already struggling with not getting enough sleep each night and going downstairs to eat was already a nightmare, so to live through home improvements while I ate is something that I will never be able to forget from the way it had further impacted me.

The male parent would always know when I would be downstairs, but I would have to wait until he was finished doing whatever he would be doing. This is understandable when there is work going on, but his behaviour was completely unacceptable!

There was a time where I had just prepared my food and had sat down to eat when he thought it was a good idea to start power flushing the radiators and if you have been present when radiators have been power flushed, then you will know the kind of smell it creates!

Did I say anything about it to him? I didn't, and it's because my youngest brother was downstairs and from various experiences where the male parent has made it seem like 'I was the problem', there was no way in hell that I would give him the satisfaction of being seen as the victim, especially after the 24th June 2016 incident when he lied in front of the police by saying, 'you are a harm to my kids'.

I wasn't going to allow him to turn those lies into the truth, so I stayed quiet and ate my food while knowing that one day, karma would visit him and leave him feeling a lot worse than he had ever left me feeling!

When I asked the younger male sibling who was eighteen at the time about the 'For Sale' sign, he began defending the male parent by telling me that he wasn't abusing anyone and then denying the abuse that he was witnessing me live through!?

He was fully aware of what was happening to me and he knew that because of me, he didn't become homeless the previous year, so it hurt me so much to realise that he had also started gaslighting me just to protect himself and that makes him more of a coward than both parents put together.

What made me so angry is that I had conversations with him about why the male parent was so desperate to sell the house and the fact that the male parent was willing to disturb his younger kids education by taking them out of school before they had even completed their final years, he was only thinking about himself.

Every few days, the younger male sibling would tell me a different story about their plans and they never made any sense? There was one story that took me off guard completely and the younger male sibling still didn't stand up against the abuse that I was experiencing.

You may wonder and think that he was only eighteen and may have been afraid, so why would I expect him to speak up? It's because he was an adult while being fully aware of what was happening and instead of helping me when he saw just how vulnerable and broken I felt, he stayed quiet and allowed the abuse to continue right in front of his eyes while then denying what I was experiencing.

This was after he had admitted that he agreed I was being abused the previous year, around the time I had been financially abused to save the parents from losing the house that they took the risk of just to try to have me back into their control.

Put yourself in this scenario for a moment and imagine that you are eighteen years of age and you have an older brother who saved you from becoming homeless where you would have struggled so much and at the same time, you are witnessing that same older brother being emotionally and psychologically abused by your parents. Would you speak up, stand up and do whatever you could to stop the abuse, or would you stay quiet and allow it to continue?

I wasn't expecting him to do anything major and all that I hoped for was that he would stand up for me and question both parents about their behaviour because if they kept saying that they 'loved their kids' and were doing everything to 'protect' them, then why would they emotionally and psychologically abuse the 'son' that had always been there for them!?

The story that took me off guard involved the younger male sibling telling me that the house they would buy wouldn't allow him to go to a college near the house, so him and the father would stay in a hotel for the weekdays and then only be home for the weekends?

I don't know about you, but if you were buying a new house to live an easier life without a mortgage, then why would you think that this idea was the best solution possible!?

Everything that I was hearing didn't make any sense, and those stories were simply a way to keep me vulnerable and distracted from reporting them to the police. This is because they knew that if I felt that my youngest brother would be in any actual danger, then I would have taken that risk and reported them!

What I couldn't understand was how the male parent felt that selling the house was going to be achievable when he had a lot of home improvements to get done that was going to take a lot longer than just a few months?

It wasn't even possible because he didn't have much money to do it and he would spend any spare amount that he had on materials and there wouldn't be much food in the house. A few weeks before the home improvements had begun, I had overheard two conversations between both parents and that's when my theory of why the male parent was so desperate to sell the house had become slightly clearer, but it would still take me a few more weeks until I knew the actual reason.

The first conversation involved the male parent telling the female parent that how they were living wasn't okay and the fact that the female parent would go to work in the afternoon and come back at night wasn't okay.

The second conversation involved the male parent telling the female parent that if he put the house up for sale, then he could tell me that I needed to look for my own place. As always, during the second conversation that I overheard, it involved him cursing me, which wasn't a surprise.

After finally realising that there was simply nothing that I could do and after feeling completely broken to the point where I became physically sick and started to lose weight, I decided to see what I could do in terms of finding my own place.

I first went to my local council, and they told me what I already knew they'd tell me. Just how I would look for a place to rent on my own privately, they would do the same thing except a lot of paperwork would need to be filled out first.

I also felt completely helpless and alone because I had broken down in tears and told them that I was being abused, but they just asked if I was okay?

It was 2018 after the Domestic Abuse Law came into power in December 2015, so they really should have called the police, especially as it's their duty with being the local council who helps the public!? The entire environment inside felt so depressing and that's not even just my thought because it's literally that kind of energy that you experience.

The person who I spoke with even told me to lie to landlords and say that I was working when I was on social security to get a flat while knowing that I would be breaking the contract and that would lead to me being evicted!

They work for the local council who is meant to help you get a place to live in, yet he was telling me to lie that would make me homeless!? It's no wonder people do whatever they can to stay out of the system and that's something that I completely understand now because once you're in the system, it can feel impossible to get out of.

After realising that it would be easier to find a place on my own and a landlord who wasn't part of an estate agent because I was still on social security at the time and estate agents don't always accept people on social security, including most independent landlords, I started looking on various websites to try to find an affordable flat to rent that wouldn't put me in financial struggles.

There were so many that I looked at all over the United Kingdom and I just wanted to find one that was affordable with the town and city not too far. In my first memoir, ALMOST, I described how, when looking for a course on the college website at the end of 2013, The Prince's Trust Team Programme kept lighting up as if a Guardian Angel was giving me a direct sign to say, 'this is your next stepping stone'.

Well, the same thing happened when I was looking for a flat and it was literally everything that I had envisioned in the past! I always hoped to live somewhere that had a walking distance into town and a thirty-minute train ride into the city and that's what I had finally found, so it was simply perfect!

The only thing that I was hoping for was the landlord accepted people on social security and after a few days of wondering whether I should have left home during that time or not, I decided to pick up the phone and find out.

It felt completely surreal because it was the 20th September 2018 and on that very same day in 2016; I called the DWP – Department for Work and Pensions to find out whether my application had been accepted, so I could begin self-employment as a life coach and here I was now finding out if I could get a flat that I really wanted?

One major life lesson that I received from this experience was knowing that whatever you envision that brings you peace and happiness, it ends up happening when it's meant to and sometimes it's actually a teaser of what life will be like because every time I had envisioned something; it felt like I was seeing it unfold visually and now I realise how accurate it was!

It was now the 21st September 2018, the day before my twenty-seventh birthday, and the male parent's abuse got all too much once again that lead to an argument with the female parent and younger male sibling both present.

During the argument, the male parent admitted that 'he took my money because he wanted to and he shouldn't have done it'. He also admitted that the eldest male sibling 'did confess' to abusing me while asking me whether it was him or not as 'he was possessed to abuse me' when the reality is he had abused me because that's who he is!

The younger male sibling had now heard the confession from the male parent's mouth and as my entire mind and body was filled with several emotions and feelings that I couldn't handle, I started crying so much before walking into another room as both of the parents followed me.

The look that I saw on the male parent's face as he followed me is a look that I am very familiar with and it's all about taking advantage when I am vulnerable to have what he wants.

The first red flag was both parents being really calm and nice, like they cared about me because a narcissist is only ever nice when they want something. The red flags that followed involved the male parent telling me that if I went with them once the house was sold, then he would buy me a house that was mortgage free because 'renting isn't safe' and this left me completely confused.

He also said, 'who's going to look after your mum and younger brothers once I'm in prison?' Instantly, I knew that he was still trying to keep me in his control and the real reason of his desperation to sell the house was because he wanted to make sure that he got what he wanted at whatever cost and it's what he had planned since I was sixteen years of age!

What he said during the argument confirmed it because when I told him that I had visited the council and they said there is no council housing available for me, he replied with, 'I know you're not going to get a place'. He was fully aware of the circumstances that he had left me in and this allowed him to almost successfully manipulate me to achieve what he had always set out to gain.

His desperation was stronger than it had ever been and I had learnt another life lesson; I was never going to be able to work, save money and then escape while I lived there because I would be seen as nothing more than just a house slave who was a resource than a human being.

What they weren't aware of was the day before, I had phoned a private landlord and we had agreed to meet on the 28th September 2018, so I could view a flat that would potentially become something that I could finally call home!

The day had finally arrived, and I made sure to wake up early, so I wouldn't miss the train. I had never travelled to the place I was visiting before, so I was both excited and nervous.

I decided not to eat breakfast in the house when I woke up because that would mean seeing both parents and I didn't want to see them that day, so I left earlier to make sure that I gave myself some time to eat at the train station.

I was still feeling physically sick, so I wasn't able to finish my breakfast and this was one of the things that kept me motivated to escape as I was so eager to finish a meal and actually enjoy it!

Once I had finished eating, I walked around the train station and looked for the platform where I'd be boarding my train. All I can say is that I am so glad that I did and I love the mindset that I have always had of being at least thirty minutes early because I was waiting at the wrong part of the train station.

I couldn't seem to find the platform and my train wasn't showing up on the departure boards, so I asked an assistant and they had made me aware that I needed to walk over to another station that it was connected to and that's where I would find my train.

Finally, I was at the right part of the train station and waited close to the platform where I would be boarding my train, so I wouldn't miss it if I ended up having a funny thought of walking around to pass the time.

During the first part of the journey, I drafted a blog post that I would post on my life coaching website on a weekly basis and while writing it; it helped me to understand life a little easier and realise that it's always best to take things as they come and to always be open to whatever changes may occur because let's be honest, life won't always happen in the ways that we want it to as it will happen in the ways it's needed, so we can achieve what we are born to accomplish.

I don't think that I thought about the past much during the second and final part of the journey because I was somehow able to keep my focus on looking forward to what could be?

I knew that I was born for a specific reason and even though I still couldn't understand that back in 2018, it slowly became easier to understand that after I had escaped. However, I still kept an open mind because there was still a lot of uncertainty about what I was really meant to do, as I wasn't meant to know every detail until that chapter in my life had ended.

One thing that I accepted was that life is more fun when it's mysterious because it gives you a wonderful adrenaline rush as you think about all of the wonderful things that could go right rather than always focusing on what had gone wrong.

It's quite interesting how life continues no matter what is happening and I guess that's the biggest reassurance, right? That we too, as humans, can continue just like life does because no matter how dark the days might be, we will see and experience brighter ones!

It was around early afternoon when I had reached the stop that I needed to get off at and then I walked from the train station to the flat. The landlord was already waiting in his van and we then went inside and spoke.

I had written down several questions before that day and had also read various articles and guides on what to look for and ask when viewing a place, so I was already prepared. This is something that I have always done because even though I have learnt to go with the flow, preparing myself enough for something so important is essential!

If I remember correctly, we spoke for at least an hour and for the first thirty minutes; I wasn't feeling good about the place. It wasn't because it wasn't perfect; it was because I kept feeling like I needed to deal with my past before starting a new life.

At that point in my life, I had become very spiritual, so I kept asking for spiritual guidance on what I should have done, and I didn't have to wait long until I knew.

I instantly thought, 'what if you go back and the house gets sold and you then have no place to live!? You would need to go with them and they would achieve what they have always wanted while you will suffer for the rest of your life! You will not get a better deal than this and the landlord is willing to help you in ways that you couldn't have ever imagined! You haven't been eating and you need a safe place to live because that way, they won't get what they want and you will still be able to achieve what you have always wanted! If they are not around you, then they can't stop you from living your life any longer, so please just take this flat and sign the papers because you might not find a better deal like this again anytime soon!'

I told the landlord that I would take the place and in that moment; I paid the deposit before exchanging further details and knowing what else I needed to do. The best part about it was that when I spoke with him over the phone on the 20th September 2018, he told me that there were no issues with me being on social security, so it was more about visiting the place and if I liked it?

'Now you can breathe, Shikesh', are the words that I instantly told myself! I couldn't quite process what had just happened because I had been wanting to escape since 2010, when I was eighteen years of age and finally, at twenty-seven years of age, it was happening!

Walking back to the train station felt so amazing and I admired the surroundings because it's such a beautiful place. I kept thinking about all of the possibilities and I couldn't help but smile.

Finally, after feeling like I had no control over what was happening, I felt on top of the world because the parents weren't going to get what they wanted and I wasn't going to tell them that I was escaping as I would leave them to find out for themselves.

All of the emotions, feelings and thoughts of negativity had left my mind and body and it made the journey back so peaceful where I felt completely calm! It was something that I hadn't felt in a long time and no matter how unbearable the following week would be; I knew that it wouldn't last forever because I was finally going to be escaping and they would never see me again, just as I had told the male parent in September 2017 when he had financially abused me again!

From the following day and until the day of my escape, all of my focus went into changing details on legal documents and packing. I made sure that I didn't make it obvious of what was happening because I knew that if the parents had found out, then they would have played every mind game imaginable to stop me.

No matter how unbearable it was, I couldn't wait until the day of my escape had arrived, which felt like an entire month because time travelled so slowly! Instead of feeling angry about it, I learnt to cherish that time until the day of my escape because I knew that I would never experience the abuse from them again!

This is what kept me going in the times of uncertainty because I still kept feeling like I should have stayed and dealt with the past, until I would reassure myself of the reality that I was living. After all, just because I wasn't there any longer, it didn't mean that they had gotten away with how they had treated me.

I remember the evening before the day of my big escape and I was still physically sick, so I didn't eat much apart from a packet of crisps while I was sitting beside my youngest brother as I thought about how I would say goodbye to him, but as I didn't quite know from how emotional I was still feeling, I had decided to let it happen however it would play out because I didn't want to cry that evening.

Potential buyers had also visited during that same evening and I remember thinking, 'I am so glad that I won't have to experience this chaos ever again!'

The day of my big escape had finally arrived, and it was the morning of 6th October 2018. I knew that my driver would arrive with his van at 9am, so I decided to put everything downstairs thirty minutes before. That way, I could just load everything into the van to make life easier because I literally had such a small amount of stamina!

While I was bringing everything downstairs, I heard the male parent tell the female parent in Gujarati, 'Shikesh is leaving'. They both came rushing out of the living room and the male parent asked me if I was leaving?

I simply ignored him while just looking at him before walking back up the upstairs to continue putting everything downstairs. The female parent then walked up the stairs behind me before she stood in the corner half way while the male parent was downstairs touching my suitcases as he said, "Shikesh, why are you doing this, mate?"

I was completely speechless and decided not to say anything because I knew what he was all about! It didn't help that I almost fell down the stairs twice because the female parent wouldn't move even when I had told her to move a few times!

While I walked down the stairs again, my eyes locked onto the male parent and I told him that if he continued to touch my things, then I would call the police in that moment before looking at the female parent as I walked back up the stairs. I simply told them both that they needed to stop lying and admit what wrong they had done because the only people they were truly lying to was themselves!

The male parent then told the female parent in Gujarati to go down and let me leave peacefully before he told her to wake up their younger kids.

As I looked at the female parent, all I felt was pure rage because during the argument on the 21st September 2018, she had told me that she had never been domestically abused and I gave scenarios of the kind of beatings that she had experienced which the male parent kept denying by giving me evil looks and raising his voice over mine.

I even went down on my knees with my hands together and literally begged the female parent to speak the truth, but she still kept denying everything, even though the look on her face showed nothing but guilt!

After I had finally put everything downstairs; I sat on the bed that I had slept in for the last time and turned on the fan because I was sweating and completely out of breath. Over the years, I hadn't noticed just how much stamina I had lost due to all of the abuse and on the day of my escape; I became fully aware!

The male parent decided to get ready and leave in his car. I had no idea where he had gone, so I was concerned that he would wait somewhere and then follow me to know where I was moving to and that way, he could still try to control me, but I didn't let that bother me too much because if he had become aware of where I was, then I was fully prepared to hurt him and finally stop him for good!

It was now 9am and my driver still hadn't arrived, so I waited and waited until it was almost 10am and he still hadn't arrived!? I gave him a call, and he was at home before realising that he had got the times mixed up, so he made his way over to me instantly.

Once he had arrived, I told him not to tell anyone where we were going if they had asked him before he helped me to load everything into the van. During the journey, he became aware of why I didn't want anyone to know.

Once everything was in the van, I went back upstairs to check once more that I had taken everything and I kept experiencing a strange feeling like I had left something behind, even though I knew that I hadn't. It was a similar feeling to when people go on holiday and they feel like they have left something behind, but I think for me, I still couldn't believe that I was actually escaping, knowing I would never return!

During all of the abuse that I was experiencing, I overcame many fears, but the two main fears that I still had to overcome were living alone for the very first time and then finally being able to work and pay all of my own bills while making sure that I didn't struggle financially.

I knew that I would overcome both fears because at that point in my life; I had become used to taking care of myself, so I knew that it was completely possible and even though I had never had a paid job before, I felt confident in knowing that one way or another I would always be okay because I never stopped believing.

For that moment on the day of my escape, the only thing that mattered was never looking back because it was the start of a new life and one that was completely free from abuse, or so I thought.

The only thing that was left to do was say goodbye to my youngest brother, and I didn't care a lot about saying goodbye to the one that was eighteen. I was really conflicted about how I felt towards him because he had already shown me that he didn't care about the abuse that I had experienced right in front of his eyes.

If he had cared, then he would have said something to both parents and furthermore, he would have come up to me and asked if I was okay or if there was anything that he could do to help me!?

As I was severely emotional and wanted time to understand the anger and betrayal that I felt towards him, I didn't say anything about how his actions had made me feel, so I spoke to him like there were no issues.

After saying goodbye to my youngest brother and closing the living room door, I felt that I needed to say one more thing that was really important for my youngest brother to know and that was to not trust what his parents may tell him about me and why I had left because they were the reason and not any other reason that they would give to him. I also told him that he would understand everything better when he was older.

I also decided not to hug my youngest brother because saying goodbye felt impossible enough. To carry a memory of hugging him for the last time while knowing that I wouldn't see him again would have had us both in tears in that moment and it may have angered me so much more to the point that I may have cancelled the plans before killing both parents.

Finally, I had escaped and the journey to my first ever home felt so exhilarating as I thought to myself 'eight years later and you have finally done it!'

Chapter Two

It Must Be Done

My first night's sleep in my home was so blissful and as I was completely exhausted from the day of the escape, I slept really good! It had been a while since I had slept so well while feeling safe and sound, even though I was still living with so much anger.

Before escaping, I had decided that once I had settled in, I would sign off of social security and find a job because I knew that the amount of social security I was receiving, it wasn't going to cover all of my expenses.

But after realising that I would only survive a few months on the money that I had saved, and I wasn't going to secure a job right away after being turned down by more than twenty places that I had applied to, I decided that it would be best to move onto Universal Credit from Employment and Support Allowance.

I had chosen to do this because after speaking to the DWP; they had told me that in order for me to claim housing benefit to help pay my rent, I would have to go onto Universal Credit.

I remember my first meeting with my work coach and, as I had mentioned, that I was self-employed at the time as a life coach; she needed to see all of my records since I started my business to confirm that I was being honest and also had the legal side of things covered.

She looked through everything and knew that I had done everything that I needed to do in terms of having business insurance, filing a yearly tax return and so on, but that meeting made me feel so alone and unheard and it didn't make it any easier as I was putting all of the papers back into the file while she sat and watched.

When people say that 'the environment inside of a Job Centre is like people are judging you', that's exactly what it felt like! My agreed commitments in order to receive Universal Credit were to continue building my life coaching business while looking for part-time work to support myself.

At the time, I had thought to myself on how long it would take me until I had secured a job? I was fully focused on finding a job as soon as possible because I disliked every moment while being on social security from having to keep explaining myself yet not being heard. I mean, how hard can it really be to secure a job? For me, it felt impossible!

I had originally planned to unpack my things over two weeks however, as I needed to print off a few documents for my first meeting with my work coach, I had unpacked everything within two days and it had made things easier because I could then focus on everything else that I still needed to do.

It truly amazed me how quickly I had got into action from the first day of my escape and I guess now as I think about it, I had never left 'survival mode', so that's what I was doing; still surviving.

My first ever job interview was at a betting shop and I wasn't surprised when I didn't secure the position because I already knew that I didn't give my all during the interview. I guess it wasn't meant to be though because from how the events in my life would begin to unfold within a few months, I fully knew that I wouldn't have been able to keep the job and would have had to go back onto social security that would have made me feel a lot worse!

Before even attending the job interview, I felt so broken by knowing what my reality was and all I wanted to do was scream because every time I had gotten close to doing something before I had escaped, my plans were always pushed back as I wasn't seen as a human being, but just a piece of trash to throw away after the parents had got what they needed; every single time!

I had also already written and edited my manuscript for ALMOST, but after my escape, I was uncertain about what to do about the end of Chapter One. In the end, I was fully happy with how I had brought it to a conclusion and as I thought that my life coaching business would slowly start to build, there was nothing more left for me to say.

I also felt incredibly empowered as the publication date got closer. It almost felt like I had recovered from everything and could then begin living while not being triggered by the past.

It was a similar feeling that I had experienced when I launched my life coaching business, so I felt complete bliss in knowing that I could still experience that kind of happiness. It was a huge reassurance that I desperately needed, so experiencing it was literally my life line!

One major thing that I had realised was that my goals kept expanding, and they got bigger by the day. I had thought of a long-term plan on how to build my success in order to solidify my legacy, but it wasn't long before I had realised that my life was going to take another turn within a few months.

After all, and majority of the time, nothing has ever happened without a major struggle in my life and that's something I have accepted now.

The day of the publication had now arrived, and it felt completely surreal! On the 28th November 2011, I had phoned for an ambulance to be taken to hospital as I was suicidal and on that same date in 2018 – seven years later; I published my memoir.

I thought about that day and realised just how many times I had become suicidal in order to find the truth and now that I knew the truth, there was nothing more left for me to do in order to have closure because being able to still live my life would have allowed me to experience closure in every way that I could.

The amount of pain that I experienced within those seven years has taught me so much about myself as a person and by knowing that I made every decision with so much thought and planning, it is what saved me a lot of guilt and regret because not once had I put myself first and it was essential that I didn't put myself first.

This is because if I had done, then my youngest brother would have been taken into care where he could have possibly been abused himself and that is something that I couldn't have ever lived with, so for all of the times that I didn't do anything to physically defend myself or report the parents again before my escape, even after the

Metropolitan Police Force had already failed me, it was for my youngest brother's safety no matter how much I had to suffer along the way!

My suffering had slowly become bearable, and it remained a daily motivation for me because it had shown me that nobody could ever change who I am. This is what kept me going because I know who I am while being completely happy with who I am and if others don't accept me for it, then it's not going to make me feel any less.

It had now been a few months since I had moved onto Universal Credit and when I attended my appointment with my work coach; she told me that her colleague would join us in the meeting as she had looked over my file and realised that I had moved onto Universal Credit from Employment and Support Allowance while being depressed, so some extra support would be helpful to me.

This really stopped me in my tracks as they say because, after feeling like I was all alone in terms of support from the Job Centre, she helped me to understand that I wasn't.

In the meeting, I shared my journey of how I had got to that stage in my life and why I had to escape as they both listened. This then led to a conversation about further support and how an organisation would be able to help with getting my confidence back while also helping me to secure a job. I thought to myself, 'I have got nothing to lose', so I decided to accept the extra support and see where it would take me?

After a few weeks of waiting. I finally heard from the organisation and an introductory appointment was then set. I remember it very clearly because while I was sitting in reception, I looked around and kept thinking, 'I have been here before!'

It was a feeling that I have experienced many times prior to that day, so it was something that I was used to. You might be wondering what I mean by, 'I have been here before?'

Well, my life has led me to becoming a very spiritual man and with everything that I have experienced while seeing various events in my life unfold how they have done, I believe that I chose to be born with this life while knowing what I would experience in order to make the changes that I have already made and will continue to make. I had started to let go of the fear and fully invest my trust in the journey because deep down; I know that everything would always be okay.

There have been various moments in my life where I have experienced déjà vu immediately after a certain event and I believe that déjà vu happens to give me the reassurance of knowing that I am walking on the road that I am meant to be on according to my life purpose.

After waiting in reception for a few minutes, I got shown around the office and introduced to various different people who would support me at different stages of the programme, which would last around a year. As they were aware that I was self-employed at the time, a meeting with the self-employment advisor was set.

From feeling supported and heard, I once again felt unheard and silenced, but maybe my goals weren't meant to happen how I had imagined? Maybe I was only meant to be introduced to that organisation to attend various confidence and self-awareness classes while also being aware of further skills that I held? Could there have been a different reason?

My appointment with the self-employment advisor didn't impress me because instead of him asking me questions to get to know me and my business better, he simply asked questions that I already knew the answers to, while also making a comment about 'how I looked younger, so people wouldn't want to hire me as a life coach'.

Even though I didn't feel helped by the self-employment advisor, he did mention a conference that himself and others had put together that I could attend as it may help me with meeting people who could play an important role within my journey of raising awareness about abuse and how survivors continue to struggle, yet those who are guilty continue to have their freedom while abusing and destroying many more lives!

The conference that I attended was about child sexual exploitation and it involved survivors sharing their stories while various professionals spoke about their experiences of helping survivors with getting justice and making changes to the system.

It was such an empowering event, and I spoke with various people who helped me to understand what more I could do with what I wanted to achieve in terms of getting my voice heard.

It was this event that gave me an entirely new insight into what was going on with many other survivors and how they were also let down by the authorities.

This is where I started following many survivors on social media that opened up so many powerful conversations because there will always be an ongoing concern as no one should ever have to experience any form of abuse!

During this time, there was an enquiry going on into the failings of the police forces and survivors were being encouraged to speak up and share their stories, so any investigations that ended with a 'No Further Action' could be looked over again.

I decided to send my memoir to them, but as the months went by, people slowly realised that it was just a 'publicity stunt' that wasn't meant to do much, but only make it seem like changes were going to happen.

A police officer had emailed me and he enquired whether I had any further information to give to him in regards to the incident when I almost got run over by the neighbour in my childhood? It was way too late to even do anything about it, so I emailed back and told him that there was no point because I didn't have any further information.

I had almost secured a job while on the programme with the organisation, but in the end, it wasn't for me as I wouldn't have done it for the rest of my life. I was only looking for a part-time job to help support myself while I continued to build my life coaching business. The job was for a care assistant within an elderly care home and I had passed the interview successfully!

However, the taster day is what allowed me to realise that it wasn't for me because after seeing the various care assistants at work while I supported them in some of their duties that I was allowed to do, it reminded me of who I am and what I stand for. I have always believed that if you're going to help someone, then help them all the way, otherwise don't even bother to start!

I would have worked over the weekends only and when I saw how the residents communicated with the care assistants and asked them about events that were happening in their lives, I had instantly decided that I couldn't take the job because only working on weekends just for money wasn't part of my morals and values.

After all, it wasn't just a job; it was a service that involved caring for the elderly in such an empathetic and sensitive way, so I couldn't see it as a job, I just couldn't!

It had now been a few months of receiving support from the organisation and I had begun feeling even more alone. The main advisor that I had, she had left the role as she was starting another one, so I was then being seen by another advisor.

I felt heard and supported at first, but it slowly turned into being made to feel like my voice didn't matter and how 'my plans' were unrealistic just because I wasn't securing a part-time job and had said no to the care assistant role because of my morals and values?

That's how it felt anyway, even though she didn't use those words directly, but the way she spoke made it feel like she had done.

During this time, I was given another work coach at the Job Centre and from the first day I spoke with her; she showed me just how much she cared and understood what I was saying.

It felt like I could tell her anything and she would understand, so that's what I did, I told her that the advisor in the organisation I was being supported by was making me feel alone and as my mental health had started deteriorating from continuously remembering the 24th June 2016 incident and how my life would have been different if what needed to happen had happened, including how traumatic my escape was, I was being told that 'I needed to be around people' when really, I needed to be alone and to rest from how tired I felt.

This is when I stopped attending the programme and, as my work coach at the Job Centre was aware of my overall health, she advised me that it would be best to hand in fit notes after getting them from my doctor.

This would then lead to a Work Capability Assessment to determine if I was fit to work or not and if I was fit to work, then by how much and what could I do?

I had one of these assessments all the way in 2011 when I signed onto Employment and Support Allowance on the day I almost took my life where it was pretty straightforward and after the assessment; I was left to rest and get better.

This memory helped to reassure me of knowing that I would be understood once again and given the time to get better before being able to look for work. Even though I knew that it was going to be straightforward, I wasn't looking forward to it because I would have to go into detail about why I wasn't feeling okay and speaking about the past has always been severely triggering.

It had now been a few months into 2019 and I became aware of just how severely my mental health was affecting me. I would have nightmares every single night, and it would feel like they were real.

I would wake up in cold sweats, filled with anxiety, begin to panic, not knowing where I was and the biggest thing that helped me to understand just how urgently I needed support was waking up literally screaming and shouting because the nightmares felt that real!

I had decided that I would try to keep my mind occupied for two weeks and to look after myself as best as I could to see if I felt any better, but even after two weeks, I kept feeling worse.

This is when I started thinking about reporting the parents for the abuse that they had put me through and if it was the only way to face the past in order to destroy it completely, so it would never affect me as severely ever again, then I was fully prepared to do whatever it took because this time, my health was more important than having fears of what would happen to my youngest brother?

The truth is, I was brainwashed to always feel guilty and fearful of being blamed and that always stopped me from doing what was right and this is what allowed the parents to continue abusing me while knowing that I was in their full control and they could push my buttons whenever they wanted, so for that reason, I will never be to blame for anything when I have never been the problem!

I have always expressed that 'feeling dead inside while you are still alive' is one of the worst feelings that you can ever experience and that is what I kept experiencing. It wasn't worth it any longer from how severely I was being triggered, so finally, I had to do what I needed to in order to help my overall health.

It was Monday 1st July 2019 when I reported the domestic abuse over the phone. Describing the details of several events over a twenty-year period made me realise just how much I had lived through and no matter how many times I may have spoken about the events, it still leaves me shocked from how inhumane it all was.

It was either the same day or the next when I received a phone call and spoke with a police officer to arrange an appointment for me to give a formal statement and hand over all of the evidence that I had to support my case. On the day of attending the police station, I spent the earlier hours before my appointment reflecting over everything that had happened while double checking everything in the folder to make sure that I had everything together and wasn't forgetting anything.

The day felt quite surreal and as I look back now, the day of every major event that has happened in my life has felt very different. Whether I knew what was happening that day or I would come to know about what was going to happen, it always felt different. It's a feeling that can't be explained, as it can only be experienced.

I reflected over just how far I had come and kept questioning why everything was happening the way it was? Why did I have to reach a point where waking up screaming and shouting needed to be the wake-up call of realising that I couldn't just carry on trying to build a life when clearly the past was still in my present?

As always, I reassured myself by knowing that everything has always happened for the greater good, so whatever was going to happen once I had reported it, it was also for the greater good.

During the meeting with a police officer who took my formal statement, I went over all of the events since I was seven years of age and even though I had written a memoir that was already published during that time, it still blew my mind from just how much had happened. Describing the events in full detail and experiencing every emotion that was linked to the events wasn't just a walk in the park.

It took up to two hours before my statement was fully typed up and then all of the evidence was signed and sealed before being ready to send to the Metropolitan Police Force.

I remember leaving the police station and telling myself that it was finally done and the amount of freedom that I experienced of not having to carry all of the weight from the past any longer allowed me to finally sleep without waking up screaming and shouting.

One thing that I kept thinking about was what would happen to my youngest brother because before I left the police station, the police officer told me that he would request a 'welfare check' to be carried out and that made me panic a little, but I didn't worry about it too much because it was out of my hands.

It was now the beginning of August 2019 when I received a phone call from a police officer within the Metropolitan Police Force. He introduced himself and told me that he had requested my formal statement and evidence that would take a few days or weeks to be with him, so if I had digital copies, then I could send them to him and he would get started on it right away.

I tried sending everything in several emails, but as I was sending several documents, my email was being blocked. I then decided to create a Dropbox account and send the link to him so he could download everything that way. After it was sent, I never received a confirmation email back? I assumed that he had read it and was getting on with investigating my case.

It had now been a few months, and I hadn't received any replies to my emails and the times I had called, his mobile phone would always go to voicemail.

I can't remember if I had left any voicemail messages and there were times where I would get an automated out of office email that would state that he was on training days and so on. What I kept questioning was that I hadn't heard back at all and that had me feeling like something was wrong? I decided to phone the non-emergency phone number – 101 and find out that way because surely someone could give me an update, right?

I spoke with someone who informed me that nothing had been done my case and the investigating officer's line manager had left a note of concern on my case file questioning why nothing had been done? It felt like my entire world was falling apart all over again because I was slowly feeling better, but after realising that nothing had been done to my case for a few months, it took me right back to the 24th June 2016 incident and I felt completely neglected all over again!

During the same phone call, it was suggested that I could file a formal complaint while I was on the phone and everything would then be addressed by the investigating officer's line manager.

After hearing that I could file a complaint, it instantly took me back to the 24th June 2016 incident because I wasn't even aware that I could file a complaint if I felt something had gone wrong! I had thought that the word of the police when they are called out is the final outcome. This enraged my anger to another level because I had a right to know about this information in 2016 that would have changed everything!

I can't remember whether it was the same day or the next when a police officer phoned me about my complaint, who reassured me that I had every right to be angry because he would feel the same way if it had happened to him. Before he got off the phone, he told me that the

Metropolitan Police Force doesn't use Dropbox, but a similar service called Box.

That same evening or the next around 7pm, I received another phone call that I couldn't answer and once I could; I listened to the voicemail to see who had called? It was the investigating officer's line manager and while I spoke with him over the phone, all I heard was him making excuses without telling me why my case hadn't been worked on?

The way he spoke with me clearly showed that he wanted to close the complaint as quickly as possible and it made me feel so alone, like I didn't matter to them? Like many other times in the past where I have become completely silent because I couldn't speak from how traumatised I had become, I experienced the same thing. All I wanted was an update and there I was finding it really impossible to accept that nothing had even been done?

Before getting off the phone, he told me that because the Domestic Abuse Law came into action at the end of 2015, any events prior to it wouldn't be looked at, which puzzled me because no other police officer had told me this specific information? I had thought that once domestic abuse had become a law, then any events prior to December 2015 would also be investigated?

This is where I questioned if it was even worth continuing with the investigation because the abuse began when I was seven years of age, so if those events wouldn't be looked at, then it was pointless to have the events after December 2015 investigated as it wouldn't be a complete investigation.

I decided on what to do by telling myself that I had already started it, so I might as well keep going because I needed closure in order to move on and it felt like I would experience it with the help of the criminal justice system?

From the further distress that had been caused, I had self-referred myself to therapy and was put on a waiting list where I then had two or three meetings with different therapists to complete all of the relevant assessments. Once they were all completed, I was put on another waiting list until it was my turn.

I had also begun to experience severe back pains while my right hand and lower arm began having nerve problems. I was referred to a physiotherapist after the initial consultation for my back pains and for the nerve problems; I was referred to a physiotherapist who showed me a few exercises to do at home for a few weeks before meeting with him again to see how I was doing.

As the exercises had made the nerve problems slightly worse, I was referred to a private hospital to get the nerve problems checked out before being referred to another hospital where surgery was going to be the possible outcome.

The remaining few months of 2019 felt so uncertain, as I wasn't just living through a nightmare from being re-traumatised and further distressed by police officers, I was also experiencing various medical problems while waiting for therapy to begin.

I also began feeling distant to my life coaching business and from how vulnerable I had become; I began thinking about stepping away from it because I couldn't continue wasting money on keeping it going when clearly nothing had come from it.

I found it really hard to even think about because I had written my memoir, ALMOST, in such a way that made my life coaching business feel like a certainty that made me question if I would have to re-write, ALMOST, because it didn't seem like it was okay to leave it the way it was if I did step away from my life coaching business?

As always, my spirituality helped me when I needed it the most and after a lot of meditating and looking for answers, I decided that if I did step away from my life coaching business, then I would simply write a second book that would continue from where I had left off at the end of Chapter One.

It also seemed like a second book was needed because after reporting the domestic abuse, my story was clearly left unfinished and, for that reason, it was left untold!

Many things had happened from the end of 2019 to the beginning of August 2020. The outcome of the Work Capability Assessment didn't go my way because they felt that I was fit enough to do some form of work, even though I had described just how much my mental health was struggling.

I had a month to have the decision reviewed, but I decided to first see if I could help myself get better, but my mental health kept going downhill to the point where I started to have very dark thoughts. It was only then that I decided to have the decision reviewed, but the outcome remained the same, so I then applied for a Tribunal Hearing and was now waiting for the date.

During the wait, I attended physiotherapy appointments over the phone for my back pains and was guided through various exercises to continue doing at home that would slowly strengthen my back.

Therapy for my mental health had also started and from attending the sessions face to face, they continued over the phone because the entire world had shut down from COVID-19.

The lockdown for me as a whole was a blessing because it gave me the time that I needed to fully rest and make the right decisions in my life that were really needed. It's where I started to come together with who I really am and stopped pretending like my life was normal.

I cancelled the Tribunal Hearing as I began to slowly feel better by doing one important thing that I hadn't done much of for a very long time, and that was giving myself a break.

During the beginning of 2020, I had applied for a Therapy Administration Apprenticeship that I didn't secure and, after feeling better; I had applied for an IT Engineer Apprenticeship that seemed like I was going to secure, but once the lockdown had come about, the role was no longer needed and my appointment for the nerve problems got pushed back, so I continued waiting, but from how the world was living, it was uncertain when I would hear back and receive a new appointment.

One of the biggest decisions that I made was stepping away from my life coaching business and I felt ready to do that because it wasn't what I wanted any longer and I felt so relieved after making that decision as it removed a lot of the stress that I was carrying.

It was during this time that I completed therapy for my mental health. I was given twelve sessions in total and only completed eight of them, as I had reached the stage of feeling like myself again. Throughout the sessions, I had addressed several things that weren't addressed in the past, as I wasn't ready to face it all back then, but now that I was ready, therapy helped me to understand just how much I wanted to become a DJ and a music producer that slowly allowed me to grow the excitement for it again. I told myself that even though it may not have been something that I did as a career, it's something that I could still do to keep healing.

Finally, my passion for life started to grow, and everything was going okay again. I began making even more changes to my life, from starting to eat a lot healthier to exercising regularly while keeping up with my back exercises to continue strengthening it.

Within the complaint that I had filed about the investigating officer, I had asked for another police officer to investigate my case and after we had initially spoken in either December 2019 or January 2020; she had updated me in February 2020 when I asked for an update. I came to know that the male parent was questioned, but it was now August 2020 and I hadn't received an update since then, so I had assumed that COVID-19 had pushed the investigation back as it wasn't seen as urgent?

My patience couldn't hold on any longer, so I decided to phone the investigating officer during mid-August 2020 after sending her emails and leaving voicemails where I received no reply at all, but she answered my call this time?

I informed her that I hadn't heard back and when she told me that she had emailed me months ago about the decision; I had no words. In that moment, it felt like it would have been better to kill myself because another police officer had caused me so much distress and this is when I had sustained permanent injuries, but it would take me until 2022 in order to understand the severity of them from how further events would unfold.

After hearing that my case had been closed months ago, my heart had sunk and my entire world fell apart because I received no email, no letter and no phone call to inform me that the investigation had ended with a No Further Action!

For two whole days, I experienced the kind of darkness that I have never experienced before and even though I had been suicidal several times in the past before that moment, what I experienced in those two days was something even darker!

I had thought about revenge, killing myself and continuing my fight through the legal system very carefully during those two days and in the end, I decided to do what was right; to file a complaint against all three police officers to the IOPC – Independent Office for Police Conduct.

I kept thinking about all of the delays in the investigation up to that point and it made me realise that whatever the outcome would have been, I would have known either prior to starting therapy for my mental health or while I was already in it, but therapy had been completed and there I was feeling like I was back at the start line!

During one of the therapy sessions, I remembered an incident that happened to me around the same year when the eldest male sibling had sexually abused me in the health club swimming pool.

I don't remember the date or the time of day, but I do remember what specifically had happened and after so many years of wondering whether if it was a 'normal behaviour', I have finally accepted that it was far from normal.

It was outside of the tennis court inside of the health club where I was waiting for the class to finish, as it was my class next. Suddenly, I froze completely because the male parent had grabbed my right butt cheek really hard. It felt like his nails were digging into me.

The pain remained for a few days and when I got home, I took my pants off and checked with a hand-held mirror where I noticed bruises and one or two of them seemed like some blood had been drawn. The pain and bruises remained for up to two weeks before they were gone.

What could I have even said at that time? I had already been told several things that kept me in constant fear, so to even think about bringing it up was out of the question! I can't remember if anyone had seen what had happened, and I wondered if there were any cameras around that area? No one had said anything to me, so it seems like there wasn't anyone around when it had happened?

For many years, I wondered if other parents did such a thing to get their child's attention and it was only in 2020 when I finally destroyed that uncertainty.

There isn't a single form of abuse that the male parent hasn't put me through and I don't even know how to feel about that realisation!? How can someone be so dark hearted towards an innocent, helpless child? I will never understand that because there is not a single reason in this entire universe that would justify an adult abusing a child!

It was sometime in September or October 2020 when a police officer had phoned me and informed me that she would be investigating my complaint.

During this time, I was applying for apprenticeships and came across the same one that I had applied for at the start of 2020, but hadn't secured it. When I applied for it the second time; I felt a lot more confident and truly believed in myself.

What I was also aware of was that I wasn't fully ready for the role, but because I had become severely suicidal from knowing that another police officer had neglected me, I was doing everything that I could to give myself a reason to continue living.

As I thought about how my life would change if I ended up securing the apprenticeship, I smiled at the thought of being able to have a full-time job, being able to save more, eventually putting a deposit on my own house within a year or two, signing off of social security completely and finally living my life just like I had always wanted to!

After a few weeks and on my twenty-ninth birthday, I received an invitation via email to be interviewed for the position, which made the day even more special! I literally couldn't believe it and it still didn't seem real, even on the day of the interview. I was really shocked during and after the interview because of how confident I was that I witnessed myself.

There was also a very important lesson that I had learnt before the interview and it was about reaching out no matter what because I had come down with a flu before the interview date and the interview was meant to take place face to face. On the page where I selected the time for the interview, it stated that if I couldn't make the interview, then I would need to cancel it and would sadly lose the opportunity to be interviewed for the role.

It was a very uncomfortable thought of knowing that I could lose the opportunity just because of a flu, so I decided to call the administration team that gave me the answers that I needed because I realised that they would still be happy to interview me virtually!

As I had already spoke to one of the manager's at the start of 2020 to find out what the outcome was of my application, she had got to know me a little better and that's why reaching out is so important because otherwise, you won't know how else something can be done and what support is available that can be offered to you.

I didn't have to wait too long after the interview because after an hour or so; I received a phone call where I was offered the position! I was so emotional and almost began crying because of how much I wanted it and finally; I had been offered the opportunity to work in an environment and with people that cared about people! I honestly couldn't have been given a better opportunity during that time!

There were still a few things that needed to be done before I could start the role, such as doing a background check, speaking to the references that I had given and having a phone appointment with the employee health and well-being team.

This is when I went back in time to 2014 and remembered just how hard it was to get onto The Prince's Trust Team Programme. I reflected on how dedicated I was and would do everything that I could to make sure that I achieved my goals.

I also had to order replacement copies of my BTEC First in Business Certificates that I had completed in 2009, as I didn't have them any longer. This gave me a chance to remove the middle name from them and it felt like being awarded them again that felt amazing.

Finally, all of the checks were done, and I started on Monday 2nd November 2020 and got into the role very quickly! Even though it took me some time to learn the new systems that I had never used before, it didn't feel impossible and I began enjoying each new day that kept teaching me even more to help me succeed further.

I was also told that I could complete a Leadership and Management Coaching qualification that would be fully paid for and after having an initial meeting with the person who was in charge of it, as I would be supported by him throughout my apprenticeship; I felt even more excited about my future and where it could take me! I was absolutely blown away by all of the doors that were opening up for me and every single morning, I couldn't wait to start working!

Do you know when you watch movies and shows where everything is going so well and you think to yourself, 'wait, why is everything going this good?'

Well, only after a few weeks, my mental health began struggling from various triggers and this began affecting me more than I could handle. My sleep started to suffer, and it kept feeling like I didn't have any control because I had no self-awareness of what was happening, both emotionally and mentally. All I knew was that how I was left feeling by another police officer, the distress that I had tried to block out completely had risen to the surface.

I spoke with my managers and took a few days off while also speaking with the employee health and well-being team. Even after a few days off, I still felt very vulnerable and didn't know what was happening, so I decided to take an unplanned annual leave for three weeks that I felt so bad about because my line manager had arranged her annual leave and would need to come in after all.

I hated what was happening and after thoroughly thinking about what I needed to do to help myself and also put my colleagues first; I had no other option but to terminate my apprenticeship because my mental health was deteriorating at an extreme rate and I couldn't be around anyone.

During my first week on the apprenticeship, my elbow appointment had finally come around that I had attended at a different hospital than the one I was working at. It wasn't a huge problem, but it would have been easier if it had been at the same one where I was working.

I spoke with a consultant of the surgeon who explained how the surgery would have been done and the risks that I could face such as it still not being better where it could get worse and also the possibility of a serious infection due to COVID-19 that could have killed me!?

As my elbow wasn't affecting me a lot and it was slowly healing on its own, the consultant stated that the risks were too high and as it wasn't as bad as when I first had it checked out, it would be better to let it heal by itself. If within six months it got worse, then I would simply need to call him and a surgery would have to be done. Thankfully, it slowly healed by itself and didn't affect me any longer.

From everything that seemed like it was going so well, my entire world had become so broken and I wasn't able to have any control over any aspect of my life. I referred myself to intensive psychotherapy.

Usually, I would be able to have some self-awareness about what was happening with my mental health and the form of support that I would need, but this time, I didn't, and that's what made it even scarier. I also wasn't able to help myself like I normally could, and that added more to the confusion that I kept experiencing of not knowing what was happening?

After having the initial assessments, I slowly began to understand what was happening. Even though I had a slight idea while I was working at the hospital, I still wasn't fully certain about my theory.

When the role involved answering the phone, certain types of tones in people's voices and the way they'd speak if they were frustrated, it began triggering the times I was being domestically abused. It started to feel like it was happening all over again and kept getting worse by the day. The 24th June 2016 incident continued to give me extreme flashbacks that refused to stay silent.

What I didn't realise is that I would have to wait until the police investigations were completely over in order to start therapy because otherwise, I would only keep being triggered and the work that would be done within the sessions would be a waste.

This is what I had originally thought and didn't know what to do, but in the end, I was happy with the conclusion because now it was about facing the past one step at a time than trying to build a new life when I was still stuck in the past.

During this moment in my life, I questioned why therapy in the past had only worked for a short period and I had now understood that it was because I had only dealt with the moments when I was in crisis. Even though I had addressed past issues, I had never fully dealt with the trauma intensively to reshape the way I thought and felt about it all.

This also included processing all of the trauma and working through it all, but at the time, I was still living within it all even after escaping, as clearly the journey still wasn't over.

It might seem like a small realisation, but for me, it felt like the biggest lightbulb moment because I was now able to understand what needed to be done, how it was going to happen and when, even though the exact date wasn't known.

I was given a few referrals that I could do as a short-term solution, so I was still supported and being helped, but before I could make the most of them, chronic insomnia starting ruling my life. In the past, I would be able to get my sleep schedule back in shape in one day by staying awake and then falling asleep at night, but this time, it wasn't possible no matter how many times I had tried.

This is when I realised that if I had forced myself to stay on the apprenticeship, then I would have had to leave no matter what, so this gave me peace in knowing that I had made the right decision. Even though it was an impossible and emotional decision, it was the right one.

While experiencing chronic insomnia, I also began comfort eating where I would order takeaway food two to three times a week for three months and this is when I knew just how low I was feeling. Even though I had spent a few hundred pounds on takeaway food during that time, I was happy that I was able to eat than feeling physically sick and losing weight, so that meant more than anything.

I also saw it as a positive thing because before escaping, I would always lose weight from losing my appetite, so the fact that I was eating and enjoying it a lot, it kept my energy levels up and allowed me to always stay focused on what was happening that always led to thinking logically and not letting my emotions completely rule me.

Throughout the police investigation of the complaint against all three police officers, I began realising just how neglected I felt from the amount of questions that I wasn't asked. Not only was I left alone to continue wondering how the case was progressing, but I was also made to feel like I had been forgotten.

The police officer that was investigating my complaint was taking me completely seriously and every question of mine, including everything that I had to say, it was being heard and replied to fully. Finally, things were starting to go my way and the further the investigation progressed, the more heard I felt.

There was a time where I had asked the police officer that was investigating the complaint on whether she knew about the welfare check and if it had been carried out? I explained what I was told when I first gave a formal statement, so I wanted to know if a welfare check had been carried out to make sure that my youngest brother was okay?

I was told that nothing had been stated on any documents and in order for a welfare check to be carried out, there would have to be a cause for concern and as they didn't have any because they hadn't received any reports of harm and so on, legally they wouldn't be able to do anything. This is when she suggested that I look up my youngest brother on social media.

I couldn't find my youngest brother on any social media, so I then searched the address, and this is when I realised that they had sold the house and had moved to the place within England where the male parent had always planned to move since I was a teenager.

My heart literally hurt so much because they were now living mortgage free! I was severely abused since the age of seven and being thirty-two years of age as I am writing this, my life has been on hold and I have been struggling more than they have ever done! The amount of abuse that I have to work through each day is enough to kill anyone!

I knew where they had moved to because the male parent is a plumbing and heating engineer who is self employed, so his tax details for his company are for public record.

But are they really happy? This is something that I have asked myself for so long. There is no way that they are truly free and happy because when you have abused someone for several years and then lied about it by not speaking the truth, that stays with you every second of every day!

It took me a few months to process everything about both parents being free from financial worries, but what brings me peace is knowing that karma will knock on their door one day. They can run anywhere in this cruel world, but they will never be able to hide and the fact that I ruined the male parent's plans by finally reporting everything to the police, any crimes that they may commit won't just be seen as them being the 'innocent ones'.

The male parent is going to grow old and be all alone just how his father was and the two biggest fears of the male parent have always been being alone and growing old and dying, like his father did. The only difference is his death will be worse by knowing that he tried to show his parents how he was different from his other siblings, yet he turned out to be a lot worse than all of them put together!

The memory that he will never be able to erase is thinking about his father and instantly seeing my face and hearing my voice because I was so close to his father. Everything that I did with him will haunt him and when his final days arrive, the pain will be extremely unbearable by knowing that he will be going somewhere a lot worse where he will never be able to stop the pain.

For the male parent to think that I wasn't brave just because I saved my youngest brother from ending up in the care system by not taking the risk and reporting him to the police before I had escaped, it makes him nothing more than a coward because there is no bravery in abusing a child! He abused me since the age of seven while he treated his other kids how kids should be treated with love and care.

What I have lived through and have overcome is something that he couldn't handle for a single second and the kind of strength that I have has allowed me to not use violence because it would have helped him and destroyed me. Instead, I focused on my future by knowing that I was willing to take the short-term pain in order to have the long-term freedom.

When you have abused someone for many years who has done nothing wrong to you and especially when they have saved you from being homeless twice with many other scenarios that would have left you completely destroyed, you are never free and are always paying the price with the memories getting stronger every single day!

Every action creates a memory and no matter how bad you try to remove it, that memory stays alive for as long as you are alive. I have accepted that they will pretend to be happy and put on a fake show in front of everyone that walks into their life, but one way or another, who they truly are will never remain hidden because the truth always comes out in the end.

During the complaint investigation, I had told the police officer that my medical records hadn't been obtained and, for that reason, I wanted the domestic abuse case to be opened again. After coming to an understanding about this, she had agreed.

Before the case was opened again, she explained that another police officer would be assigned to the case and the three police officers that I had complained about wouldn't contact me or have anything to do with the investigation.

Once a police officer had been assigned to the case, we had spoken on the phone for about two hours and as the weeks had then gone by; he had mentioned to visit me in order to carry out a video recorded interview, so I wouldn't have to keep talking through everything. This is because if the case was to go to court, then the jury would be able to watch it without me being in the main courtroom, so I wouldn't have to face the parents.

After knowing that I wouldn't have to be put through the whole cross-examining that I have heard so many horror stories about from many survivors, it helped me to feel reassured.

I had also mentioned that I wanted to press charges against the female parent also because without her full support, the male parent wouldn't have been able to abuse me so severely and for the length of time it went on for.

The one fear that I had about my youngest brother ending up in the care system no longer remained present because he would turn eighteen years of age the following year and, for that reason, he would be an adult!

The video recorded interview was initially scheduled for the 12th July 2021, but as the police officer wasn't able to find a colleague who would be free to assist him, it took place the following day.

From February 2021, I was living with chronic insomnia and it still wasn't any better, so I am really glad that the text notification was able to wake me up because even my loud alarm wasn't waking me up, so I must have been in a light sleep.

I didn't think that the text message would be from the police officer because I had emailed him the previous day in the afternoon and hadn't received a reply of whether the interview would be taking place on the 13th July 2021 for definite?

After reading the text, I had realised that him and his colleague were on their way and would call me around 12pm if I wasn't already awake. I got up and prepared myself emotionally as quickly and as safely as I could before speaking with him over the phone.

As I had at least thirty minutes before him and his colleague would arrive, I began moving things around to free up as much space in my flat as possible for the equipment to record the interview and then sat down to help myself be as relaxed as I could be.

The night before, I felt so emotional and wanted to cry so much that didn't happen in the end and now that I look back; it makes me wonder what really exists in the afterlife because crying during the video recorded interview wasn't planned and it just happened, yet before that day, I would only cry at happy moments or when watching a really powerful movie that would overload me with so much emotion such as the movie, The Lovely Bones.

Speaking about the trauma wouldn't make me cry either, even though I felt that I would break down any moment, yet it never happened before the day of the interview apart from when I was on the apprenticeship. I slowly started understanding how I had been left impacted with permanent psychological injuries once I had realised that another police officer had neglected me.

No matter how emotional I may have felt before the day of the video recorded interview, I wasn't able to physically show it and even my anger felt trapped, no matter how angry I felt every single day. The way I was abused for several years, including the way the police officers had left me feeling themselves, it made me realise just how alone I have felt majority of the time.

The video recorded interview lasted around three hours and I went over as much as I could in full detail, with me breaking down in tears while explaining Monday 28th November 2011, the day I would have killed myself.

One thing that I was made aware of was that the female parent wouldn't be charged separately if it would go that far as she didn't act alone, so she would be charged alongside the male parent for supporting him by staying quiet and emotionally abusing me at the same time. I was okay with this because that's exactly how it was.

The next steps followed with gathering the medical evidence and then analysing it all to see if it would be enough to back the bank statements with the diary images being mentioned as supportive evidence rather than being used alone. This is because it wasn't strong enough alone, as I didn't have the original diaries and only the pictures of the separate pages.

I was told that it couldn't be used alone because if it was to go to court, then both parents could claim that it wasn't written by them. It's reasons like this that make me realise just how broken the system is kept to let abusers continue abusing while those that have been abused continue to struggle to stay alive.

It had now been two months, and I received a phone call from the police officer on the 16th September 2021. I guess you can say that my reaction wasn't fully normal. How a person would be severely triggered and all over the place, I was completely the opposite after realising that the case would be closed with a No Further Action!?

How could the evidence not have been strong enough when the bank statements and diary entry images supported each other!? In 2016, before having the diary entry images, I questioned how I would be able to carry on living if both parents were to ever get away with everything and here I was asking myself that very same question!?

Around this time, I had received an email from an organisation that had informed me they had partnered with a law firm and would send all enquiries regarding personal injury claims to them.

My emotions still weren't making me feel completely broken, so I had assumed that not reacting the usual way that would be expected was my actual reaction and I had accepted the outcome, so it was now time for me to start letting go?

I thought about my next steps and had decided to claim personal injury compensation with the help of the law firm, as it would help me to get my life back on track.

As I was now aware of my next steps, I called my doctor and referred myself to therapy for my mental health, as I knew that no further investigations would be happening. It was during this time when I began reflecting over the therapy that I had received during the moments of crisis that led to being even more self-aware.

My goals for the future were always bigger than my pain, so I never truly understood how I was really feeling on the inside. It made me question whether it was normal to not have the usual reactions that a survivor tends to have?

This started to change when my goals for the future became uncertain and once that had happened, all of the pain that I hadn't experienced yet had risen to the surface and that made me realise what had really happened.

One major thing that I had also decided to do was to start letting go of the anger fully because it kept me in the mindset of wanting to choose revenge. By knowing that the parents had got away with everything, it continued to torture me every single day, but I then had to understand that they had never got away with anything.

This is because I spoke about what had really happened and they had to face the reality that all of their secrets and lies had been exposed where they could no longer hide behind them. My focus began to slowly shift after understanding and accepting this, that then helped me to start thinking about the future once again.

But it wasn't long until I began having a mental breakdown and the outcome of the investigation had started to cause me so much distress that receiving the compensation made it seem like the abuse was still in control of me.

I had filled in all of the paperwork and it was ready to send to the law firm, but from the breakdown that I started to have the night before, I realised that I wasn't willing to go ahead with it because my mood swings became so severe that I felt so lost and broken.

I spoke with the lawyer at the law firm who was going to be dealing with the claims, and we agreed that I would take a few days to rest and think about what I would choose to do.

In the end, my decision was to not claim it, and I was reassured about this choice after receiving a phone call to arrange a mental health assessment prior to starting therapy. This made me realise that I was ready to finally move on from the past and the pain completely in order to start building a new life from where I was.

On Wednesday 20th October 2021, I had my mental health assessment over the phone and it felt so good to get it all out again, but it also made me realise just how much trauma I had experienced within a few months.

It's definitely not something that the human body and mind was built to cope with, so experiencing triggers very often is completely normal and I wasn't afraid to express just how hurt I was because I had finally stopped acting like everything was normal when it wasn't.

This is how I would always have to behave before escaping, and it was completely draining to have to keep putting on a fake mask around the cowards that didn't care about me.

On the 14th December 2021, I had my follow-up therapy assessment and on the 21st December 2021; I received a letter that stated what the next steps would be.

The therapist felt that I needed some talking therapy first and to complete a few online self-help courses to help with my chronic insomnia and triggers to not feel extremely angry when speaking about the past. This is because EMDR therapy – Eye Movement Desensitisation Response that is a form of cognitive-behavioral therapy; it could have become too much for me to handle.

Once I had completed talking therapy, I could then refer myself again to have EMDR therapy if I still felt that I needed it. At first, I felt confused about why the original plan to be offered EMDR therapy didn't happen? But I also felt that I was being redirected and had to keep the faith, as everything has happened for a reason.

I was going to wait until the New Year to contact the organisation for male survivors that would help me with receiving talking therapy, but I decided to do it on Christmas Eve.

Instead of waiting, I wanted to get going with things because I was tired of waiting around. Luckily, I was able to have a video call the same day, and an appointment was then booked for the 4th January 2022 that would involve filling in forms prior to starting therapy of twenty sessions.

I also contacted another organisation to sign up for the self-help courses and awaited to hear from them. After taking these steps and being proactive, I still felt like something was missing, especially after the video call because I realised that in order for me to fully let go, I had to do something that I didn't think was necessary, but clearly it was, and without doing it, I would have always felt held back from reaching my highest potential.

Even before the video call, I kept feeling like something was missing, so rather than waiting any longer, I called 101 on Boxing Day and reported the remaining events of child sexual abuse against the male parent and eldest male sibling. The reason I hadn't reported the remaining incidents of child sexual abuse was because of the way that they happened and the amount of shame that was involved where I felt I wouldn't be believed.

While I was on the phone explaining the abuse, I started to dissociate really severely and it felt like I was in a daze. It's something that I had never experienced before and it almost felt like I had broken some form of control that it had over me?

I also decided to ask about whether a case that had gone to court and ended with a no guilty outcome could be investigated again, especially if I knew what had really happened?

I was told that I needed to speak with a solicitor, but I decided to contact The Crown Prosecution Service directly to get their response. I tried calling on the 27th December 2021, but there was no answer, so I decided to leave some feedback via their website and waited for a reply.

Once The Crown Prosecution Service had emailed me and after I had provided them with all of the details that they had asked for, so they could then address my enquiry fully, they had forwarded it to the right office, so I then needed to wait until the New Year for a response.

One major dilemma that I struggled with for a few months towards the end of 2021 was trying to understand whether I wanted to become a therapist or not? I had come to know about a Level 2 – Mental Health Awareness Course that I could do from home for free, as it was fully funded by the government. As I needed to focus on something new, I decided to sign up for it.

The course covered many aspects of mental health and I also learnt about various laws that allowed health professionals to deliver the best care that they could and reading about how the treatments for mental health have developed over several years was very eye opening.

After completing the course, the dilemma that I had been faced with had now been solved because it showed me that any roles that involved supporting people from experiencing abuse, it wasn't something that I could do any longer.

As I had started to slowly let go of the past fully, I felt that I needed to do something different because supporting people during the day and also working through my own demons at the same time would only drain me to the point that I would end up leaving, anyway.

Gaining this self-awareness allowed me to look forward to whatever 2022 would bring, and I couldn't wait to see the year unfold. Whatever I would be doing and however I would be doing it, it wasn't going to be a problem because I would finally be free to live my life with nothing stopping me from becoming the person that I was born to be!

This is what I had hoped for, but what I would come to understand is that my journey still wasn't over and once I would begin therapy in February 2022, I would come to understand several things that would lead to some major life decisions; the kind that was going to leave me struggling even more than I had already done.

Chapter Three

The Ultimate Sacrifice

Tuesday 4th January 2022 had finally arrived, and I had a video call with the male survivor organisation that I would be receiving talking therapy from. I had shared the decisions that I had made, such as filing the remaining crime reports and how good it felt to have taken more control over my life.

During the second half of the video call, the forms were being completed and when we had got to the question about any disabilities that I was living with; I mentioned my mental health as I had come to know that mental health is seen as a disability and then I spoke about a possible learning disability with numbers as I wasn't fully sure if that was the case or not?

I was reassured a lot and even given a new alternative as to why I may find it difficult to deal with number solving problems that aren't simple and it could simply be because of the abuse that I have lived through since a very young age.

This is something that I had never even considered before and it wasn't something that someone had even mentioned, so it was a huge wake-up call of beginning to understand how the abuse has affected the way my mind processes information.

Abuse can affect a person's entire life in every way and make things feel impossible to achieve when, for others who haven't experienced abuse, they can find it really simple to do everyday things such as driving a car even. This took me back to when I was learning how to drive and I really disliked being on the busy roads.

From remembering this, I started to put everything together and realised that the chaos in my head was always so loud, so having to deal with real life learning felt impossible majority of the time. After always wondering why many things felt so difficult to accomplish, I now had a bigger picture to look at, even though it had always been in front of me!

This is what abuse can do to a person where it will completely block them from seeing the truth until the cover is finally lifted by experiencing the lightbulb moments from being heard.

By knowing that the person I was on a video call with was also a survivor, it gave me so much more reassurance from being guided correctly while being asked the right questions. When you are being supported by a survivor led organisation, it not only allows you to feel heard and be seen, but it also allows you to heal without further setbacks that can happen from being supported by those that are not trauma informed.

The final thing that they shared before our video call ended was that therapy doesn't always need to be used to speak about the abuse because I had done a lot of that already, so addressing the things that were stopping me in the present moments could help me to build a new life.

This helped me to understand that I didn't need to speak about the abuse all of the time unless there was a reason for it and it also helped me to start seeing therapy quite differently as to how I had always viewed it before receiving that insight.

After thinking through what events in the past may need to be spoken about, I decided to write a list of everything that was preventing me from living a life in the here and now to keep me on track and focused once therapy had begun, so I knew what I had to work on in order to make the most of the twenty sessions that I had been given.

Around the beginning of January 2022, when I had given the formal statements regarding child sexual abuse to a police officer who had visited my flat and after they were given; I asked him about a physical assault that I had experienced by the male parent between the ages of seven to nine. I explained why I felt drawn towards reporting it, which was from being questioned by my dentist in 2018 about why my jaw looked like it had experienced a fracture that could be seen from an x-ray of my mouth?

The police officer explained that under Section 18, there is no time limit if an injury has occurred from an assault, so a police officer from the Metropolitan Police Force that had told me there was a six-month time limit had given me the wrong information, even when he was fully aware about the accurate details!?

This made me question the outcome of the domestic abuse investigation and whether he had made the wrong decision to close the investigation with a No Further Action? After all, the diary entry images are as strong as a verbal confession, so clearly there is evidence to show that a crime had happened beyond reasonable doubt.

From now having this information, it was enough to question everything, but instead of going ahead and reporting it, I decided to let it go as I knew that solid evidence would be needed and in court, the male parent could claim that I may have experienced the injury by falling over and I didn't remember.

On Monday 10th January 2022, I gave a video recorded interview at the police station of the child sexual abuse that I had experienced from both the male parent and eldest male sibling.

There were many moments where I began disassociating while talking through the events, and many lightbulb moments were experienced from remembering just how helpless I was as a child.

I found it so difficult to accept that the male parent had abused me in every single way and when I had thoughts like, 'at least he hasn't sexually abused me', I was now trying to accept and process that he had done and even today, I find it hard to accept because there isn't a single way that I don't feel violated by that coward!

The interview helped me to realise just how much shame I had from the abuse that I experienced by the eldest male sibling and during the interview when I was asked whether I had mentioned it to anyone, in that moment and the way I reacted, it felt like I had never mentioned it.

I was completely disassociating where I can't even explain how I felt. It's like that question finally brought the shame to the surface and only as I was writing this, I could remember that I had mentioned it and it was to the lawyer that I had spoke with from the law firm the previous year when I was about to claim compensation.

Usually, I always remember who I have spoken to and about what because I have a photographic memory, so why did I feel this way and why did it seem like I had never mentioned it to anyone when I had done!?

I also couldn't remember that I am an author and I could have written it in ALMOST. Was I disassociating that much like the 24th June 2016 incident where I experienced a memory blank?

All I could do was look through the pages of ALMOST to see if I had written about it, so I could then email the police officer and let them know that it had been mentioned, but in the interview itself, it felt like it hadn't as I was disassociating so much. I now truly understand just how much years of abuse can affect a person where they have then been made to feel silenced and unseen for so long!

Before the interview ended, I was asked whether there was anything else that I wanted to say? Before I left home for the interview, I felt a deep urge about reporting the physical assault where my jaw experienced a possible fracture, but when I got to the police station, I didn't feel as certain.

When I was asked if there was anything else left to say, I felt like it needed to be mentioned because I didn't want to hold on to anything from the past any longer, so I went into it all with every detail that I could remember once I was told it was okay to speak about it.

I felt so free after and was glad that I had got it over and done with! Finally, I was taking back my control and not letting anything or anyone stop me from speaking my truth. The walk home felt similar to the one in 2019 when I reported the domestic abuse and it felt like a huge weight had been lifted off of my shoulders once again.

After getting home, I looked up the relevant details for the physical assault report that had now been made and sent them to the police officer. Over the next few days, I emailed the police officer other relevant information with reference numbers of other cases that could help the investigations further.

I had also mentioned that if the male parent was to find out that his eldest son was going to be questioned again, then he would reach out to him and warn him off like he did in 2016.

The Crown Prosecution Service had got back to me around this time and they felt that I didn't understand what they were about, which was understandable as I had mentioned the domestic abuse investigation that hadn't gone to court. After replying to their email with a further explanation of my concerns and the details that I knew of the female parent's case, they forwarded it to the unit that worked on the trial and for them to look over my enquiry.

The following day, I attended my appointment with my work coach at the Job Centre and it felt really good to have gotten out of the house again. As I hadn't seen what he looked like, it was good to finally meet him and we had a good catch up on what had happened since we last spoke in November 2022.

He made me aware that he would need to refer me for the Work Capability Assessment that I originally thought wasn't needed and after explaining what I was told by a previous work coach; he helped me to understand that the Work Capability Assessment is a requirement, so it should have happened after I had given a few fit notes from my doctor to say that I wasn't well enough to work due to my mental health.

I shared my concerns with him as when I had it in 2019; they felt that I was able to work and after I had their decision reviewed when I began experiencing really dark thoughts, they still felt that I was able to work, so I knew that I wasn't looking forward to the assessment because they clearly weren't supportive from the conclusions that they had made about my health without experiencing it themselves.

What helped me to stay calm and focused was knowing that my work coach would fully support me as he genuinely cared and if it meant that I had to take the decision of the Work Capability Assessment to a Tribunal Hearing like I would have done in 2020 if the COVID-19 lockdown hadn't happened, then that's what I was prepared to do!

On Monday 17th January 2022, I called my doctor to get a new fit note that needed to be provided to my work coach and I also booked an appointment with my doctor to have a consultation about being formally diagnosed with C-PTSD. As it was something that would remain for the rest of my life, I felt that it was important to get this done and have it formally verified and signed off by a professional.

My doctor called me later that day and explained that doing a formal diagnosis during that time wouldn't be effective because I was still recovering and going to start therapy, so rather than placing a certainty on something, I first needed to process things a lot more and then have a better understanding of how affected I truly was by all of the abuse and then the further distress that had been caused by several police officers.

On Monday 24th January 2022, I received an email from the Victim Liaison Officer at The Crown Prosecution Service that included a letter from the Senior District Crown Prosecutor.

It stated that after a person has been found 'not guilty' by a jury, then that person can't be retried for that same criminal offence ever again because there is no such process in all of the law that exists where the prosecution can do such a thing, but it would be possible in very serious offences!?

Isn't every crime a serious offence, or are we now choosing what crimes deserve to be heard and what crimes deserve to be dropped? The letter then stated that if other offences had been committed, then I should report it to the police.

What kept me calm and helped me to see the bigger picture was knowing that just because both parents had got away with the crimes, they didn't truly win because the amount that they have lost in the process is so much more than what they have ever achieved.

The pain of losing me has been severely extreme for them because their entire plan was focused on keeping me as their house slave, where they could do whatever they wanted with their lives. As this didn't happen and as they can never control me ever again, their entire lives have been a waste because every memory will remind them of me and what they have lost; a son that was always there for them, even when they didn't deserve me.

Another thing that they will have to live with for the rest of their sad and sorry little lives is being in a mortgage free house that they were only able to buy because of me while knowing that they never paid me back the money that they stole from me.

My thoughts were always about making sure that my youngest brother didn't ever end up in the care system or homeless and if that meant suffering more to stop myself becoming like those that abused me, then that's what needed to happen because it ends with me!

The only thing that remained was for the final investigations to be over that I had reported and once that had happened, I could finally start closing the past and building a new life.

On the upside, I received an email the same day that had informed me that I had passed my Mental Health Awareness Course and after it had gone through the internal verification process, I would receive my certificate, so the day wasn't all bad in the end. After all, it can only get better now, right? Well, I was very wrong!

On the evening of Monday 24th January 2022, I kept feeling like I had to report the female parent because she wasn't formally questioned during the initial domestic abuse investigation, even though I had mentioned that I wanted it to happen.

A huge part of me felt like the response from The Crown Prosecution Service meant that once the report to the police was on the system, it was enough for me to have full confidence in knowing that there was nothing else left to be done, so I could finally let go of it altogether. It would also prevent the female parent from getting away with any further crimes as a report about her of what really happened would be on the system.

It was around 11:30pm when I called 101 and spoke to someone from the Metropolitan Police Force. I felt completely alone because what I had said made full sense to me, but I understand that for someone who didn't know what had happened, they would find it difficult to understand the details because I was mentioning three different incidents that were all linked together in one way or another.

The police officer then stated that he only needed an overall summary of what I was reporting as police officers would need to come and see me that were local to me, so he transferred the call to my local police force and I spoke with another police officer.

She took further details of what I wanted to report and I then told her that rather than police officers visited me at home due to chronic insomnia, I would report it at my local police station.

The following day, I went to my local police station, and it took a while for the police officer at the helpdesk to find my report because I was meant to receive a text message with the reference number and I hadn't.

Once she had the reference number, we spoke about possibly arranging an appointment for me to go back another day and give a formal statement because no police officers were available to speak to me. Luckily, a few minutes later, she came back and informed me that police officers had become available, so they'd see me shortly.

I was taken into a separate room and I then explained what the reports were about, but they didn't take a statement because their line manager had told them to tell me that it was a matter for the Metropolitan Police Force as the offences happened in London, so they shouldn't be dealing with it?

This made me feel confused, and I explained that I had reported previous incidents and a statement was taken before being forwarded on, but this time around, it wasn't going to happen?

They recommended calling the Metropolitan Police Force and telling them what I had been told and if they still had an issue with it, then my local police force would take the statement and forward it to them. Once I was home, I changed and had something to eat before relaxing a little and I then made the phone call.

It felt like my entire energy was just being pulled from me and no matter how much strength I may have had; it was all being taken. The police officer informed me that I was treated in such a poor way because regardless of what crimes had happened including the location, I was in front of uniformed police officers, so they had a duty of care to take a statement, especially with the seriousness of the offences!

After realising this, I agreed with the police officer that I would file a complaint about it because it shouldn't have happened. We then discussed what report I was going to give and after speaking over the details, she re-opened the report from the initial domestic abuse investigation and sent a message to the police officer that had investigated the case last. Once I got off the phone, I called my local police force to file a complaint.

The next day and sometime in the late afternoon, my doorbell rang, and I was still in bed and half asleep. I got up and was trying to get myself together until there was a knock on the door of my flat.
There were two police officers that had visited regarding the formal complaint, so I let them in while apologising, as I had only woken up, so I wasn't fully prepared.

I explained everything of what had happened during the initial domestic abuse investigation and why I was now reporting the female parent after getting in touch with The Crown Prosecution Service. I then explained what the complaint was about and what I was told by a police officer at the Metropolitan Police Force about the duty of care and how it wasn't delivered.

Before they left, I updated them on the report that was re-opened and we agreed that I could speed it up by providing them with a statement there and then.

As I didn't know any further details of how the report being re-opened would progress, we agreed that if I hadn't heard back from the investigating officer by the end of the week, then I would phone my local police station to book an appointment, so a formal statement could be taken before being forwarded to the Metropolitan Police Force.

On Friday 4th February 2022, I had given a formal statement at my local police station against the female parent for the domestic abuse, as I still hadn't heard back from the investigating officer.

I had originally thought that as the female parent had supported the male parent and he had already been questioned about it with all of the evidence, including a video recorded interview fully documented, I wouldn't need to say much about the female parent apart from explaining how she supported the male parent in the various scenarios.

I slowly realised that I did have a lot to say as the interview lasted around two hours and thirty minutes, where the police officer who was taking the statement had to push back his next appointment.

What reassured me is that he was very person centered and had mentioned at the start that he had taken statements regarding domestic abuse previously, so he knew how hard they can be. I then explained how the investigation came about in 2019 and why the female parent was now being reported.

Unless I have forgotten which is very rare, he was the only police officer to have ever admit sitting face to face with me that every police force is guilty of not supporting victims of abuse the way they need to be supported and they all still have a lot more to learn in order to prevent such crimes happening.

My respect for him grew instantly because the way he spoke with me, supported me during the interview and after, everything that he had said and how comfortable I felt around him, I was fully reassured of knowing that he truly cares about serving the public and keeping everyone safe.

Once the statement was taken, I spoke with him over the phone later in the night once he had typed it all up and this is where he read through it while I helped him to understand any changes that needed to be made which he made a note of. After the statement was finalised, I submitted them via email with a digital signature before they were forwarded to the Metropolitan Police Force.

One of the biggest things that I have learnt from reporting the final crime reports is that when you have started to heal, you will begin to dissociate a lot more because rather than not knowing what is happening, you will be fully aware about everything that you are experiencing and this is how you will finally know what is right or wrong for you.

Essentially, it will allow you to make all of the right decisions for your life in order to let go of anything and everything that doesn't benefit your life any longer. As long as you always trust your gut instincts and follow your heart over your mind, then you will never find yourself regretting any decisions like you may have done several times when reflecting over the past.

Whenever I make a very important decision about my life, I always think about how I will feel about it when I reach the end of my life. If it's something that I will feel positive about and glad that I had made the decision, then I know it's the right one to make, but if I feel the opposite, then I'll stay away from it.

It's also important to reflect over the positives and negatives of every decision until you are fully certain because it doesn't matter what decision you make, it will always have an impact on other people's lives. The last thing that you want is for someone to get hurt who is innocent and hasn't hurt you that doesn't deserve to experience any hardships.

As an example, I could have taken the risk and reported everything in 2016 or 2017, but my youngest brother would have been taken into the care system. Sure, he had seen and heard things, but he has never ever been abused in the ways that I have. In the care system, anything and everything could have happened, so even though I didn't deserve to continue being abused just for his safety, it was already my 'normal' and not his.

If I was to report everything while knowing that he would have been taken into the care system, then he most definitely would have experienced several forms of abuse and that is something I would have never been able to live with, so I felt that it was better for me to suffer a little longer while knowing that I would be free for the rest of my life than to feel a short-term satisfaction and be consumed with feelings of regret and unbearable pain for the rest of my life.

I wasn't going to ever become the people that abused me and knowingly put a child in harm's way just to feel free of my own pain, even though I shouldn't have ever had to face that decision, but because I was faced with it, there was no way in hell that I would make a decision that would destroy a child's life while knowing what abuse can do to a person for the rest of their life by experiencing it myself!

This allowed me to try to move on without doing anything, but in the end, and as you have read, I had to report everything because it was the only way that I could fully break free from my past and live a happy life. Sometimes in life, it's better to struggle a little longer for the short-term while knowing that you will be free for the rest of your life than to feel free for a short amount of time and struggle for the rest of your life.

But if struggling for the short-term may lead to yours and / or someone else's death, then struggling for the short-term is definitely not worth it and you need to do everything that you possibly can do to prevent that from happening.

With so much support that is slowly being put in place for survivors, there is always somewhere to turn because one thing is for certain: you will always matter!

By Monday 21st February 2022, I had received the outcomes of all of the crime reports that I had filed and I am so glad that I was sitting down when I read the email because from the way I felt; it was enough to make anyone want to collapse from shock.

With the reports against the male parent, the police officer stated that it wasn't seen as child sexual abuse because I hadn't mentioned anything about the male parent receiving sexual gratification from his acts. This was impossible to witness as he was fully dressed when he had abused me, so the report was then lowered to a common assault, but with there being a time limit of six months, it didn't go anywhere as six months were over years ago.

With the report about a physical assault that led to a possible fractured jaw, they couldn't see the male parent being the suspect from when it happened to then having a fractured jaw even years later, so they didn't request the medical reports and nothing else happened.

With the report against the eldest male sibling for child sexual abuse, nothing happened because when he was questioned in 2016, he denied there ever being any sexual interactions between us.

It took me a few moments to process the shock of what I was reading because my reports weren't taken seriously or investigated and the police officer had downplayed my experiences by saying that 'commenting on a child's body isn't an offence'. What the male parent did was more than just commenting on my body because actual physical acts had taken place at the same time!

Firstly, even though the eldest male sibling denied everything in 2016, the new incident that I had reported was completely separate from the ones that had already been reported, so he should have been questioned no matter what as that's a requirement when carrying out a formal investigation!?

A few minutes later, I replied to the email stating that what had happened by the male parent, it could be seen as sexual harassment, so he could clearly be questioned on that charge rather than just a common assault, but this didn't go anywhere either?

With the domestic abuse report against the female parent, it didn't go anywhere because it was 'hearsay' and when I explained my disbelief to the police officer over the phone on how the evidence that was available couldn't be enough to bring a charge, including the incident on the 24th June 2016 when I was completely failed, he stated that nothing could happen and all I could do was sue the Metropolitan Police Force?

I had asked a question via email about why nothing had happened on the 24th June 2016 and I was told that it was noted as a verbal argument against the male parent only!?

This was the final information that I needed to understand that the four police officers that attended on the day had not just failed to protect me, but they had left me in an environment where I was being kept as a house slave and I could have also been killed!

The abuse that I experienced after this incident had escalated because the parents now had no fears by knowing the police officers didn't even arrest them! The amount of anger that I have experienced since that incident has been so toxic that killing myself would have always been easier and I wish that I had killed myself after that incident!

If any of the police officers had asked the male parent to allow me to speak than stand there and allow him to continue interrupting me, then I wouldn't have been left so distressed where I am still living with the distress even today.

They could have also taken me to another room and spoken to me alone because all of the signs were there to know that I was being intimidated and had been persistently targeted while being so vulnerable. They didn't even give me any information on what would be happening next or any information on how I could file a complaint if I wasn't happy about how they may have handled the incident by failing to not follow and deliver the Victims' Code of Practices.

I didn't even know that I could file a complaint until the end of 2019, when I phoned 101 to get an update and was then told that I could file a complaint. Before becoming aware about it, I was left to believe that the police have the final say and you can't even file a complaint because this is how lost and vulnerable I had been kept as a house slave!

By knowing that I was completely failed on the 24th June 2016, I filed a complaint about the incident and, by knowing that I was finally starting therapy; I remained hopeful of being able to process everything that had happened over the last few years.

I also didn't realise just how much I needed it until the morning after the first session. I was slightly nervous as my therapist would be someone completely new that I hadn't spoken to before, but I was also eager to speak at the same time as I had waited over a year for some therapy and finally it was happening.

The first session allowed me to vent and explain what had happened since I had escaped from London on the 6th October 2018, including what was happening in my life during that time. It helped me to reflect on just how hurt I was, but it also allowed me to see my strength and by the end of the first session, I knew that my therapist was the one that I was meant to have as she truly listened and cared.

The following day, my anger was still at its highest where I just couldn't shut my mind up from overthinking. The thoughts, emotions and feelings kept me in an internal rage for almost the entire day!

All I could think about was hurting the abusers in a way where the world would know what they had done and I was prepared to pay whatever consequences it would lead to!

I had written up a long post on Twitter and was going to expose the abusers names while mentioning what they had done and in a single second before posting it; I realised what I was experiencing emotionally, and it was the same emotion as when I have always reacted to the abuse in the past rather than responding to it where I would be in control and not my mind.

Instantly, I stopped myself from posting the tweet and calmed myself down by knowing that I would have regretted making such a decision because it wasn't going to give me any justice or closure, and it certainly wasn't going to give me back the years that I have lost!

I then thought about doing something and it was to send my youngest brother a letter to explain why I had to leave because I knew that he wouldn't be told the truth and would only come to know about it by looking me up online if he ever decided to.

It was also my way of making him aware of any narcissistic abuse that he may have started to experience and at least that way, he would become aware of what was happening because narcissists never stop hurting people and they always move onto someone else.

The only question that remained was how would I go about it because I wanted to make sure that it didn't leave an open connection for the parents to begin using my youngest brother in order to come back into my life.

It was in that moment when I thought about phoning up a few schools and colleges around his area before realising that he was still seventeen years of age and there is no way that any school would confirm if a certain student was studying with them as I could have been anyone.

Also, due to safeguarding and data protection laws, it was possible that if I had phoned the right school or college, then they would have a duty of informing the parents about the phone call which could have 'encouraged' the parents to make up some lie before forcing my youngest brother to go along with it just to bring trouble into my life as they have always lived for attention to be seen as the victim.

It wasn't long until I decided to send a letter directly to my youngest brother once he had turned eighteen years of age in a few months that had originally put me off as I felt that if either of the parents would open the letter and realise it was from me, then they would keep it from him.

What changed my mind and helped me to have confidence in doing it anyway was knowing that my youngest brother would be an adult and not under the care of the parents, so they couldn't do anything about it in terms of making up any lies of me causing my youngest brother harm.

Around this time, a survivor on Twitter that I had spoken to several times left a comment on one of my tweet's that expressed my thoughts about the parents and eldest brother getting away from justice as a court case didn't happen. Her words are what led me onto a journey that I never even thought I'd be on, 'what is justice though?'

It didn't hit me that evening because I was so emotional still, but the following morning, I felt so calm and refreshed because her words are exactly what I needed! I was looking for an answer of how I could move on in order to put the past behind me, and that was my answer!

I had always seen justice from what society is made to believe where if someone has hurt you, then you must report it and it will then involve a court case and a conviction, but because that didn't happen, it felt like justice wasn't served and the abusers had got away.

What I was now left with was a question about what justice meant to me and this led me on an entirely new journey that would take me until the end of 2023 to truly understand, but before that time had arrived, I started to see justice in a way where a person overcomes everything that life has thrown at them where they are then able to still live a happy life.

By the end of the week, I began thinking about my future and what truly mattered to me? This is when I went back in time and reflected over a decision that I had made. I thought about where I wanted to be in five years and claiming compensation would allow me to achieve one main goal within those five years.

Rather than feeling negative about the compensation, I felt positive because it would allow me to have a deposit for a house as owning my own place has always meant everything to me, especially when I was always made to live in fear of becoming homeless.

I hoped that I would be able to start working within a year and, slowly, my life would begin. But before all of that even happened, I knew that I needed to be ready for it. I also knew that I had to start accepting my reality because it would only keep me a prisoner of my own mind otherwise.

I had also remembered to keep an open mind and not form any expectations or to make things feel certain because life doesn't always happen in the ways we want it to, so rather than making my thoughts feel like a solid plan, I kept it all open as options of what I could do while knowing that whatever would happen, I would always be okay and have everything that I ever needed.

It was the evening of Friday 18th March 2022 when I experienced something so powerful that took me on another journey that I wasn't expecting at all! I mean, that's what life is about right where going with the flow and cherishing every single moment through this thing called life.

This journey that I was now on was all about letting go, and it started by addressing my anger in therapy earlier that week. I expressed to my therapist how I had come to the conclusion that no matter what I would have done in the past or present to get some form of 'justice', it wasn't going to bring back the life that I had lost.

And it also wasn't going to give back the kind of suffering that every single abuser truly deserves because in order for them to know what it was like for me, they would have to go through the exact same things and also be who I am because that's the only way they would truly receive the ultimate payback.

You might be wondering what I mean by 'be who I am'. Well, they would have to be empathetic, nurturing, calm and every other wonderful thing about me, yet as they are not me and will never be me, they will never suffer the way I have, so there was nothing else left to do apart from letting go completely and finally start focusing on myself only in order to build a life for myself.

The turning point for me was understanding what letting go truly meant because all I had ever known was trying to fight what wasn't going my way and holding onto something that was hurting me more and the longer I held onto it the worse I kept feeling.

I had assumed that letting go would mean I had given up, and that's what would always anger me because I had been called a failure by several people and that's definitely not who I am!

It was only until life itself had taken me to the point of finally realising just how much time had passed and the fact that I was living how I did before escaping where staying inside and sulking in self-pity, and by realising that I was missing out on life, I started to feel really uncomfortable about everything.

As March came to an end, I had finally reached a point where I began making the most of my self-care and not just continuing to try to walk before I could even crawl. I had got in touch with an organisation that offers mental health group sessions at no cost and no waiting list as it's a service that runs on drop in sessions so anyone is welcome.

My work coach at the Job Centre had told me about them and how I could become a group facilitator and work with them because it was what I had always wanted and he wasn't wrong.

Even though I had made the decision to not actively be involved in mental health after completing the online course, from how I started seeing life, I felt it was bearable and I could only truly know if I had given it a try.

Sadly, I had to put my plans on hold and this is when I understood that I was barely able crawl let alone walk, so I had to focus on my health only, until I had completed all of the therapy sessions and I also had to make sure that I could handle the chronic insomnia.

On Monday 9th April 2022, I needed to get a new fit note to give to the Job Centre, but I also had something a lot more important on my mind. It was something that I had thought about thoroughly and now I was ready to face it after addressing it in therapy.

When I spoke about the phone call to my doctor in therapy, it made me realise just how real the trauma was and how the triggers weren't just my imagination or uncertainty where I felt fear, no! It was completely soul destroying to fully understand how real it was and that was down to the Metropolitan Police Force.

During my apprenticeship at the end of December 2020, I felt so focused, even though I was experiencing so much distress from how I was left feeling by the police officers. However, I still had a hope that my future wasn't completely destroyed and I felt so excited about meeting someone, getting married and having my own children. It may not have happened in that order, but I remained hopeful of it still being possible.

Once I had left the apprenticeship as it got all too much for me and after then having to come to terms with my reality while in therapy, I realised the things that I wanted in my future weren't going to be possible any longer. This is something that will always hurt so much because I had to take that step of speaking with my doctor about getting a vasectomy.

This wasn't because I was ready to be in a relationship, it was because it was the only way that I could stay alive and possibly still experience some form of life, even casually, while being very close friends with someone if that miracle was to ever happen.

The way I am left with permanent psychological injuries from how much distress had been caused by several police officers, I found it impossible to stay alive by knowing that I was still connected to those that had abused me and the only way to completely destroy the connection from how my mind had processed the trauma was to cut off every aspect of them being involved that was related to their genes.

It was now the 6th May 2022 when I started drafting up a letter that I would send to my youngest brother. I knew that I would send it the following month, but as there was so much that I wanted to say, I knew that it would take me several days to write it all out, let alone even be okay with the final draft.

What I wasn't expecting was that all of the emotions and feelings that I had locked away in 2020 after another police officer had neglected me, it would all be experienced again! I was completely vulnerable and there were thoughts of suicide going around in my head, even though I wasn't suicidal or self-harming at the time.

It was simply because that's how vulnerable I was in August 2020 and I was now able to fully understand that if I had allowed myself to feel all of those emotions and feelings back in August 2020, then it remains a certainty that I would have killed myself.

Everything that I felt on the 24th June 2016 when I called the police to the house, all of those emotions and feelings were experienced also. To say that I was overloaded with emotional pain is an understatement and it took until the end of May for it all to fully calm down.

After I had written up the letter and was then reading over it, I felt like it wasn't what I wanted to say. This led to starting over that felt confusing, but once I had written what I really wanted to say, it was a lot clearer because it was about explaining why I had to leave and not trying to convince my youngest brother of what I had experienced.

I spoke about this to my therapist and she helped me to understand that writing such a heartfelt letter can be like writing a book where you write the first draft that was for me and because of that; it wasn't what should have been for my youngest brother to read. I also felt that it happened for a reason, so I could start processing the pain that I had locked away since August 2020 because I felt safe enough to then feel it.

I didn't read the full seventeen-page letter to my therapist as we ran out of time and reading the final few pages didn't feel like I needed to do that, but by reading majority of it, I understood just how much it needed to be sent and my therapist herself expressed just how sad it was to have to send such a letter when I shouldn't have had to be in the position that I was in.

It was the 15th June 2022 when I contacted the PO Box company that I had signed up with to send the letter to my youngest brother as not only would it keep my location private, but I would also have the reassurance of knowing it had been received. I had explained various details about the letter that I was sending, who it was going to and why I wanted my PO Box address left out of the return address.

The lady that I had spoken with explained that the return address is automatically included once the label is printed, but as she understood my concerns, she would cut my return address out of the label physically and then apply it.

Even though this may have seemed like such a small amount of help, for me, it was everything! The letter was posted the same day, and I then had a tracking code while knowing that I would be able to see the proof of signature once it had been received.

The following morning, I checked if the letter had been received and saw that it was delivered at 7:48am! My heart was pounding so much and it felt so cathartic because I was abused for twenty years by the male parent wanting to take revenge for his own decisions that had made him live with the guilt of not being with his father when he died on the 17th June 1999 in a hospital in India.

On that very day twenty-three years later, I would finally release myself from his evil intentions by sending a letter to my youngest brother that would explain why I had to escape and how I could never return. I also included everything that I would have said to the parents and the younger male sibling on the day I escaped if it had happened, so nothing was left unsaid anymore!

When I spoke about it in therapy the following week, that's the realisation that I had where because I hadn't said what I needed to say on the day I escaped, it was said in the letter and that's what allowed me to understand that I had finally said goodbye to my youngest brother in the way that I had needed to say it.

I also sent a letter for both parents, eldest male sibling and younger male sibling of what they needed to hear because if they felt that they had got away with everything, then the letter had definitely made them realise otherwise because even though the Metropolitan Police Force may have allowed them to keep their freedom, I will always have full control over people knowing the truth!

The best thing is that they could try to sue me if I ever chose to publicly name and shame them, but that wouldn't get them anywhere because I hold all of the evidence to show that they are guilty, yet they have nothing to show that I am lying and because of that, they would all end up having to pay me by having to sell their home!

All I kept hoping was that my youngest brother was at home when the letter was received, so he was the one that opened it, but nevertheless, it was sent and it's what I needed to do that had finally happened.

Either way, if the letter wasn't opened by my youngest brother, then one way or another, he would come to know about it as when you have kept something from someone and have to see them every single day, the lie has you acting differently and it's those things that give away the truth.

I had no control over it anymore, so it was out of my hands and the fact that it needed to be done, I was just glad that I had written and sent it because finally; I said what needed to be said without me being abused in any way and made to feel like I deserved to be dead. Even though the trauma will never heal, I gave myself the strength that was taken from me and from that moment; I remained unstoppable!

There was such a huge realisation from therapy that hit me so hard as it allowed me to understand just how suffocated the mind and human body can be with trauma and it was triggered by doing a rainbow diagram with my therapist that involves understanding the balance of emotions and how we can remain in the dark.

During the abuse, we are prevented from experiencing the normal emotions, feelings, thoughts, sensations and reactions because we are made to be and feel silenced while also feeling paralysed in every way possible, so when we begin healing and, for the rest of our lives, we will experience what we once weren't able to.

This is why the triggers can be really intense when experiencing them years later, because the chemicals in our mind and body will have become so pressurised that when the tank finally explodes, it will be uncontrollable!

It's like the mains water pipe in the streets that ends up affecting every home. But in the form of trauma, it can affect every single person around us if it isn't seen to as soon as possible!

The remaining therapy sessions allowed me to reflect over all of the decisions that I had made over the past few months and I also spoke about my inner child from what I had written in ALMOST at the end of the second chapter.

I broke down crying the way I did when I wrote it and it just goes to show how powerful it is! After the session, I fully realised that I had placed something that I loved as a child with the aim of having my inner child back when I was ready.

The way it is written, it relates to Super Mario 64 where you unlock the doors with a heart and you then jump into the paintings. After remembering the steps that I had taken to never lose myself completely, it made me feel like I had set a plan in motion to have everything that I loved once again; if I still wanted it when I was ready to build an abuse free life without any of the abusers around to stop me ever again!

Towards the remaining five sessions of therapy, I had started going to the mental health group sessions that I had to put a pause on to focus on my health only, and it all started by having to go to the doctor to pick up a letter that I needed to send to support my reasons for why I couldn't apply for compensation within the two-year time limit for the child sexual abuse and domestic abuse.

This step of pushing myself out of my comfort zone started making me hate being inside, so slowly, I began going to the group sessions and it allowed me to start building up my confidence in order to feel comfortable around people again.

There were times when the sessions wouldn't happen or I would feel too drained to go, but nevertheless, I was starting to enjoy being outside and this time; I felt free from all of the work that I had done during therapy.

Around this time, I received an email from the organisation that had offered me therapy and the email was about being on a Client Advisory Panel. I had given some feedback and stated that I would be interested in the role half way through therapy, so I simply read over the document that was attached and replied to the email to confirm that I was still interested.

After having my informal interview via a video call, I felt even more positive about my future because things were now happening that would allow me to do what I had always envisioned! I understood that the role could also allow me to speak with people in power in order to inspire change and I was so excited to begin because finally, everything was coming together once again.

The only difference was that this time around, nothing and no one would ruin my plans because I was now completely free to live my life and that was something that I had always wanted. Sure, I never should have had to struggle so much and fight to be alive, but my life has been unique, so I fully accepted that fighting for my freedom would then allow me to fight for humanity.

I may not have been able to stop the abuse or save myself when I needed saving, but with my experiences and my determination to always do what was right, I can help save others!

On Tuesday 19th July 2022, I woke up and felt so low that had left me feeling completely confused because only two weeks ago; I was feeling so positive about the future, but it didn't seem that way any longer. It felt like I was living in the past once again until I began thinking about contacting the mortgage company that the parents were with.

To find out myself what they would do if someone has reported financial abuse and whether they would be able to bring their own investigation felt so important because The Metropolitan Police Force should have been the ones to do this, but as you have read, they didn't follow all of the lines of enquiries.

I kept asking myself what would I get from contacting them while also asking myself if I was holding onto the past again, but it seemed much bigger than that. Even though I couldn't understand why I hadn't thought about it before, I guess it needed to happen otherwise I wouldn't have woke up with that being the first thing on my mind, right?

Now that the email was sent, I waited to hear back and just wondered what would come from it? In that moment, I felt reassured that I had done the right thing, as I started to feel positive again and one of the biggest things that I have learnt is when you make a decision that you feel right about, you begin to feel positive again, and that's your reassurance to know that you have done the right thing.

Later that day, I also felt that it was necessary to message the estate agents where the person worked who took pictures of the home in 2018, and I had told him that I was being domestically abused. The pain of his reaction and just leaving me there without calling the police kept eating away at me, so I felt like the only way to overcome it was by having it addressed myself, as he wasn't questioned as a key witness.

As I hadn't heard from the mortgage company and as I kept feeling restless and impatient; I decided to give them a call to discuss the email that I had sent and the person that I had spoke with stated that the email had been processed and would be with the relevant team as he wasn't able to see the details of the email due to the nature of it. He then gave his sympathies before suggesting that if I still hadn't heard back from the team it was with by the following Monday, then I should send a follow-up email and hopefully they would then reply.

As I still hadn't heard back, I sent another email and after still no reply; I called again and finally I received a call back from someone. To cut a long story short, they had no records at all!? I was in complete disbelief and wondered how that could even be possible?

I was certain that the parents were with the company until the end of 2019 when they sold the house and the fact that I was financially abused in September 2017 when they were given a repossession order after a court hearing; it hadn't even been five years, so they should have had records?

Every business, company, organisation and so on are required to hold records for six years and in some cases it would be ten years, so the only conclusion that I could come to was that either the parents kept lying to me about who they were really with or the company themselves had been destroying records without following the rules.

Before even contacting the company for the very first time, I had made sure that I was looking at the right company from remembering their name and logo that I would see on the letters when being financially abused, so the only way I could further investigate what had really happened was to contact the Financial Ombudsman Service who deal with all complaints against anyone that offers financial services.

Once that was done, I contacted the DWP because I kept thinking about what possible investigations they could carry out if financial abuse had been reported? Sadly, they couldn't do much because of how long ago it had happened and they usually deal with benefit fraud rather than historical financial abuse.

It's quite mind blowing how being proactive can help because I had a major lightbulb moment about how the parents could be proven as liars and enablers of child sexual abuse. Both of the parents have always acted like the eldest male sibling wasn't even with me, so if he wasn't with me, then this suggests that he was with them on a weekend break while I was left at home at the age of twelve.

If the Metropolitan Police Force actually cared and fully investigated everything, then the bank records of the parents would give them everything that they needed to know and this wouldn't just destroy their lies, but it could also suggest child negligence by the parents as they left me home alone at twelve, if this was the actual scenario of course, but it wasn't.

This is because if what they were saying was true, then questions would arise around them not being responsible parents as they would have left a twelve-year-old to look after himself and possibly his grandmother while the parents and their younger children were on a weekend break on the other side of England!

On Sunday 14th August 2022, I received the outcome letters regarding the compensation and let's just say that I felt completely disrespected. It seems like my medical records weren't even looked at because the reasons behind the amount that I was offered for only one incident within the twenty years of abuse domestic that I experienced suggested that only the police reports were looked at.

I was left in such disbelief because when I first put the claims in; I had specifically stated that the domestic abuse was mostly emotional and psychological, so they should have arranged for an assessment to be done by a mental health professional, yet I wasn't even given that opportunity.

All I could think about doing was waiting until the next day and contacting them to ask various questions in order to have an understanding of what records were specifically looked at before having the decisions reviewed of both claims. If I still wasn't happy, then I could apply for a Tribunal Hearing and then make a final decision, depending on the outcome.

The next day had arrived, and I was advised to call again the following day because the systems weren't loading and they didn't know when the problem would be fixed. Once I had finally spoken with someone, I explained my dissatisfaction with what wasn't assessed and once my questions had been answered, I then knew what my next steps were, so I called my doctor to book an appointment that I had over the phone.

When my doctor called me, I asked him whether a separate formal assessment would need to be done for C-PTSD to support my compensation claims, as the mental injuries would need to be verified by a professional.

He confirmed that the referral that had already been made in May 2022 to help me have all of the right support in place would be enough, as I had been referred to a Consultant Psychiatrist.

I was now fully reassured that I would be able to show a formal diagnosis and this wouldn't just help with my compensation claims, but it would also support me in any further adjustments that I may need to make for the rest of my life.

Now that I had all of the information that I needed, it helped me to make a decision that I was happy with. I wrote a letter for each claim to have both reviewed by giving a full explanation of why my medical records needed to be looked at.

I also mentioned that I would be attending an appointment to be formally diagnosed with C-PTSD and this would support both claims, as the assessment would explain the psychological injuries for every type of abuse that I had experienced.

Towards the end of August 2022, I received a letter from the adult mental health service that I had been referred to so I could get a formal diagnosis for C-PTSD. They stated that I needed to follow the steps that I had been given when they spoke to me last in November 2021 and this was the first time in my entire life where I have been directly neglected by the mental health services!

To say that I felt let down is an understatement because I just couldn't believe how they didn't even phone me to find out what steps I had taken since we spoke the previous year!? The thought that I had was, "do they think that I have just been sitting down and doing nothing!?"

If they had phoned me, then they would have come to know that I had worked through all of the steps that had been recommended and they would have also come to know that through the talking therapy that I had from February 2022 to July 2022, various permanent psychological injuries had been identified, and this led to taking the steps to make those adjustments just so I could still be alive, let alone even start living!

Finally, they would have understood why I needed a formal diagnosis for C-PTSD, but they just assumed that I hadn't followed the steps that we had discussed the previous year while stating that I didn't need a formal diagnosis!?

After calming myself down from the triggers that I was experiencing, I phoned them and explained that I wanted someone to call me back, so I could explain everything and hopefully, they would be willing to help me with a formal diagnosis. To cut a long story short, I was told that I was discharged from their service and because of this; a new referral would need to be sent from my doctor.

I called my doctor again, and they referred me back stating in the referral form that they needed to contact me because an assessment was essential, so now I waited again and was aware that it would be a few weeks to a few months before they would look over my referral.

One thing that I will never understand is how insensitive the mental health services can be at times and now I fully understand that no matter what type of service it is, you will have to walk through hell just to be heard!

Around this time, I received a letter regarding the compensation claims and my medical records were being requested as my request for a review had been accepted, so I phoned them to ask a few questions.

From the phone call, I was reassured that even if the mental health service wasn't willing to give me a formal diagnosis, then the team that would be assessing my claims would look over my medical records and if they felt that it needed to be looked at by a Consultant Psychiatrist, then they would have this arranged.

The following day, I contacted the various organisations that I had seen since 2020 that had offered me therapy and I also dropped off the consent form to my doctor, so all of my medical records since birth could be given to me that I then needed to send to support my compensation claims.

The amount of stress and triggers that consumed me was enough to almost change my mind about attending the Mental Health Facilitator Training with the organisation that I was attending support groups with each week because I began feeling how I did when I had to leave the apprenticeship at the start of 2021.

It felt like I was going to break down crying every single second and I was worried that if it happened while attending the training, then how would I cope with it? I decided to message them and I am so glad that I did because they gave me the boost that I needed!

After fully completing the training, I decided to take a break for the whole of September 2022 because of how tired I was. I needed to rest, reflect and gain back my strength before starting my new journey in co-facilitating peer support groups as well as attending events to share my experiences in order to continue raising awareness and breaking the stigmas of mental health as a whole.

This was the plan that I had in mind and as always, life would happen however it needed to because from one specific life lesson that I have always learnt, forcing things to happen and creating expectations when you don't know how things will unfold won't benefit you in any way as you will only be left with disappointment.

It was now the end of September 2022 and this is when I began to fully reflect over my entire life because I was now a thirty-one-year-old man. I couldn't have ever imagined how my life would have turned out by the time I was thirty-one years of age, but the one thing that I continued to feel was certainty.

I had begun to feel distant towards my spirituality over the past few months during 2022 because when the journey kept getting harder and my patience began to disappear; I questioned my existence and whether I was just wasting my time in this world?

How could I experience several years of abuse before being neglected by the authorities while they let the abusers keep their freedom that leaves me feeling completely powerless, yet I can still find the strength to find a reason to continue living?

This observation is what continued to help me walk through the dark tunnel that I kept finding myself in before seeing the light every single time.

On Tuesday 27th September 2022, I received an email from the Financial Ombudsman Service and they stated that the mortgage company had got back to them and advised that because I wasn't the account holder myself; I was seen as a third party and for that reason; they weren't going to look into my complaint any further.

My instant thought was, "how can this even be possible!? The Financial Ombudsman Service is there to take all complaints seriously against anyone that is offering a financial service to the public, so how can they then turn around and say that they are following the advice of a company that they are meant to be investigating and holding accountable!?"

To say that I felt let down again is an understatement and all I could do in that moment was reply to the email explaining my disappointment in them and how I would be openly speaking out about their services where they say one thing and then do another!?

I had filed a complaint because I had reported financial abuse and the way they made me feel was how the Metropolitan Police Force had made me feel; I didn't matter and what happened to me wasn't important enough for them to investigate.

The next step that I took was contacting the Financial Conduct Authority and told them about what had happened with the mortgage company, including what the Financial Ombudsman Service had told me. They couldn't directly help because they don't look into complaints between the public and the individual companies, but they suggested a few things that I could do.

I could contact the Citizens Advice Bureau, I could contact my local MP, I could contact the Independent Assessor of the Financial Ombudsman Service, or I could contact HM Treasury.

After thinking about everything and understanding that all I wanted from the mortgage company was to see if they could investigate the financial abuse that I had experienced, but somehow, they didn't have any records at all and then I was told nothing could happen because I was a third party, my new aim was simple.

And when the Financial Ombudsman Service didn't do anything and, rather than investigating my complaint even if I was a third party, they listened to a company that caused me nothing but severe stress that added to the distress I was already living with.

I decided to email HM Treasury as they are the government and are responsible for the Financial Ombudsman Service, so it seemed like if anything, they would take my feedback and implement any new changes, so any third parties that reported financial abuse in the future, they would be taken seriously and not turned away like I was while being given different reasons that felt like excuses.

It shouldn't matter if someone is the account holder or third party because if someone has reported financial abuse, especially when all forms of domestic abuse has been a criminal offence since December 2015 that can lead to a prosecution, then every single person should be taken seriously and not further neglected.

On Wednesday 5th October 2022, I had a phone call with a PhD student whose focus was on stalking. I had come across her on Twitter and became very interested in sharing my experiences to help her with the research because the way I was stalked, it's not something that you hear about every single day.

The phone call was originally arranged for an hour and a half, but it lasted almost three hours! I had made sure that I had nothing planned before or after the phone call because I knew that I would need all of my energy and to then rest from how tired I would be.

So much was spoken about as you can imagine and we both understood stalking in so many ways from how it used to happen to how it has evolved and the way it continues to be portrayed within the media, including in movies and shows where it isn't always accurate. Furthermore, it becomes an entertainment for people to enjoy where the conversations around how serious stalking is doesn't even occur because it's usually seen as something that happens within other crimes rather than being kept as a singular crime.

Even after the phone call, we exchanged a few emails as there were a few questions that still needed to be answered, and this is when it brought everything into perspective about just how sinister the crime is.

It was the following morning when I experienced another lightbulb moment and I had originally thought that stalking was just something that was a part of the abuse that I had experienced, but I was very wrong! It wasn't just a part that was involved; it was the main reason the abuse had happened and then continued.

This is because in order for abuse to continue happening to someone, several details about their life will need to be known and the abuser will also stalk every single person around their victims because they will try to make sure that no one ever catches them.

I have also understood how I see the words 'victim' and 'survivor'. In my eyes, a person is a victim while they are being abused, but once they have escaped and are then healing, they will become a survivor because they will never stop surviving.

We usually see stalking as someone who is being watched and followed, their phone being hacked and so on. But when do we ever see it as an ongoing surveillance operation to continue the terror that the abuser wants to inflict on their victims?

And when it comes to families where it's a very strict and traditional household regardless of the race and religion, when do we ever question that someone's life might actually be in danger and for their families wanting to know every detail about their life no matter how personal those details might be; it could in fact be that they're being stalked to be fully controlled?

The main reason they won't question it is because that's how their life may have been for so long and it has become their normal way of living without even realising what their reality has turned into.

The main reason they may not speak up about it if they come to understand that they are being stalked is because their entire families and communities may stop speaking with them and because they may not have anyone else, they remain in that cycle of abuse for the rest of their life. This is how major stalking is, and it's something that needs to be spoken about a lot more.

By realising this myself about my own life and knowing that stalking was always the main reason the abuse continued, it allowed me to see things from a very different perspective of what needs to be addressed in order to help others understand their own experiences.

For this reason, stalking isn't just a crime where someone is being watched and followed, it's an act of terror that will destroy a person's life completely and as we all have heard before, knowledge is power and when that information gets into the wrong hands, all hell will break loose!

On Tuesday 8th November 2022, I noticed that my suicide ideation had become worse and from thinking that 'it would be easier to not be in this world', I was now continuously wondering whether I even wanted to be alive anymore.

This is because the pain wouldn't stop growing and the meaning that I had given to the life that I was trying to build, it began losing its power, so once again, I had to take a step back and give myself the time to feel better.

The following day, I heard back about the outcome of the meeting regarding having help to get a formal diagnosis for C-PTSD and because I wasn't in their 'secondary care', my doctor would be the one that could provide me with one, so back to my doctor I went and booked an appointment that would take place over the phone on Saturday 12th November 2022.

Why does it have to be so hard to get a formal diagnosis? Why can't organisations and specifically those that are helping people to live with mental health be willing to help by simply offering an assessment and then giving a formal diagnosis if the assessment shows the person needs one? The sad reality is it comes to funding and unless you have money to go private, you will find yourself barely surviving.

All I seem to have experienced throughout that entire process was being pushed and pulled to the point I didn't know what would be the outcome, so I simply wasted six months waiting for replies and calling up two different people trying to get a piece of paper that confirmed I was formally diagnosed with C-PTSD.

And that's the disturbing thing about life where a piece of paper can help you, but also ruin your life, right!? If we really think about it, words on pieces of paper can cause so much harm to someone and we rely on paperwork to make the world go around. This is something that I find so fascinating and I will never be able to get over this crazy realisation.

The same day, I received an email from HM Treasury with a letter attached and it was their reply to my email. It stated everything that I had already become aware of, but it was still nice to hear back because I had assumed that I wouldn't get a reply at all.

On Saturday 12th November 2022, I had my phone appointment with my doctor and after explaining everything; he stated that he couldn't do much until he had received the letter from the organisation that I had been referred to.

He also kept stating that the symptoms needed to be worked on rather than having a formal diagnosis as well as looking at different types of therapy. This is when I realised that I was wasting my time because I already knew that the psychological injuries I am now living with are permanent and can't be helped because I wouldn't have spoken to my doctor about getting a vasectomy otherwise.

Once I had got off the phone, I emailed and updated the Criminal Injuries Compensation Authority to let them know that it would be best to start re-assessing my claims and they would need to arrange for a mental health professional to speak with me after looking through all of my medical records.

All I could hope is that this step was taken by them and I simply needed to wait until my claims had been re-assessed. However, it wasn't long until I had decided to try to get a formal diagnosis by going private.

On Monday 14th November 2022, I attended my appointment with my new work coach and updated him on how I was doing. As he had called me the week before and became aware of my mental health, he knew what sort of things I would be telling him in a private room.

My work coach had spoken to me about claiming PIP – Personal Independence Payment as it would support me further financially. I had thought about applying for it before, but had decided not to as I felt that I would have been actively doing things to help myself get into work by now, but sadly, life is very unpredictable. For this reason, I decided to apply for it the next day.

On Friday 18th November 2022, I kept feeling like I needed answers to understand why several lines of enquiries weren't followed during the domestic abuse investigation, so I decided to email the police officer that had investigated my complaint that I had filed in August 2020. After emailing her, I received an out of office reply, so I now waited until she was back from annual leave.

Later that day, I received an email from the male survivor organisation that I am supporting and it was for a radio interview to talk about a television advert that had aired by the organisation which was all about raising awareness for male survivors and the stigmas attached where males can't be victims or survivors and so on.

I felt so grateful to have been given that opportunity and speaking live on the local radio about something that means so much to me meant more than any amount of words could ever describe.

On Monday 28th November 2022, it was the eleven-year anniversary of when I would have killed myself and the day before; I kept feeling so nervous about it. It was a really strange time because I hadn't ever felt that way before around the same date, so I just wondered why it had happened?

Even on the day itself, I still kept feeling nervous, and it seemed like I had to make a decision once again that involved putting my life back on hold. I contacted the co-founder of the organisation that I had been attending mental health peer support groups with and was hoping to manage a group myself, but clearly, life was taking me in another direction.

In the message, I had explained that my mental health was playing up, and I was trying to find closure as I hadn't ever had any, so for that time, I had to step away and would contact them sometime in 2023 to let them know what was happening and whether I would still be able to help with peer support or I would be moving away from helping people for good?

To send that message hurt so much because I had really hoped that I would be managing my own group by that time, but sadly my life has never gone the way I have wanted it to majority of the time.
I was faced with the same dilemma that I had at the and of 2021 and here I was again at the end of 2022 faced with the same dilemma of thinking that the only way I could now build somewhat of a life was to remove myself from directing helping people as it was always a constant reminder of why I was doing it that kept causing triggers.

For me to be working with the male survivor organisation, it remains possible because it doesn't involve helping people directly as it involves taking part in projects, research and meetings to help improve the services for male survivors as well as art therapy and this is something that I am able to manage because it isn't a weekly commitment.

The question that now remained was what would I be able to do to earn a living when I wasn't even able to work because of my mental health? The thought that scared me was, "would I even be able to work at all!?"

This kept the suicide ideation playing up and all I could do was finally let go of trying to get my life together because it wasn't ever going to be possible without experiencing closure first.

On Thursday 8th December 2022, I received an email from the police officer that was back to work from annual leave and she would call me the following day to discuss my email. Finally, I would know what needed to be done in order to understand the questions that I had.

We had spoken for almost forty minutes and I had updated her about everything that had happened that led to discussing the questions that I had, including further discussions related to the investigations and how impossible the journey kept feeling to address the abuse that I had experienced.

After the phone call, it was agreed that the only way I could have the answers was by filing a complaint, so I did just that and there was something so important that I realised while filling in the complaint form. When I was writing about the child sexual abuse that I experienced by the male parent and how the police officer had lowered the case to a common assault before telling me nothing would happen as the time limit of six months was reached long ago, this was completely incorrect!

The first incident that I experienced involved some blood being drawn from me and when an injury has occurred, there is no time limit! This allowed me to understand that I was failed by both police officers completely that had visited me to conduct a video recorded interview, so here I was once again waiting for another complaint to be investigated and I just wondered what else would need to happen!?

As 2022 came to a close, I struggled to still experience closure and from what would be happening from 2023, it could either lead to experiencing closure in order for me to then build a new life that was bearable, or I would no longer be able to continue living.

It remained a very uncertain time and for the final weeks of 2022; I rested as much as I could because I was going to need all of my energy for what 2023 would throw at me!

Chapter Four

You Made It Personal

Once 2023 had begun, I felt so fired up and at the same time, I also felt my emotions suffocating me more than usual. This is where I had used alcohol twice in one week, so I could allow the emotions to be released, but now it wasn't helping as much.

I had started self-medicating with alcohol since 2022 where I would get drunk at home when I needed to cry because it wasn't impossible to cry when I was sober, but slowly, I could no longer cry even when I would be drunk and this is when I kept feeling like I was no longer a human being as I am not even able to even experience a human reaction and this remains my reality even today.

The same week, I had my phone appointment for the Personal Independence Payment that I had applied for and was happy that it was over and done with because speaking about everything and having to explain myself to someone who may never be able to truly understand how life was for me, it's never a nice feeling as they are the ones playing a role in the decision making of whether your life will improve or stay the same.

It had been a while, but the following day, I fainted while having a shower. My self-awareness had always been strong about how tired I would be apart from a few times, but I was fully certain that I felt rested enough to be able to have a shower; clearly I was wrong.

Once I had finally come around, I tried to stand and ended up fainting again before realising that I had no energy at all and couldn't move no matter how much I tried. It felt like I was physically paralysed. I am uncertain about how long after I was able to slowly move before drying myself and then getting out of the shower, but it was longer than just a few minutes.

This incident allowed me to realise that my health was slowly deteriorating even more and, rather than worrying myself into an early grave about it, I accepted it because fighting it wasn't going to change anything.

On Thursday 12th January 2023, I couldn't get a certain question out of my head and no matter how much I tried to let it go, it kept coming back to me, so I decided to address it because clearly there was a reason for it. I emailed the police officer that was investigating the complaint regarding the 24th June 2016 incident and asked him whether there was a time limit to report perjury and perverting the cause of justice?

After hearing back from him and knowing there wasn't a time limit as those crimes were under Common Law, I decided to contact my local police force and file those reports before they would be forwarded to the Metropolitan Police Force.

Even though the parents and eldest male sibling had got away with the crimes themselves, it was still possible to prove that they had lied during the investigations and in court, so if I was able to achieve bringing that charge, then they would receive a life sentence.

This is because lying to the police during criminal investigations and under oath in court carries a life sentence whereas child sexual abuse and domestic abuse doesn't. How sickening is that!?

On Thursday 26th January 2023, I received an emailed from the Professional Standards Unit within the Metropolitan Police Force that had the relevant documents attached relating to the complaint that I had filed in December 2022 and the following day; I received an introductory email from the police officer that would be investigating my complaint.

On Thursday 9th February 2023, I received the decision letter for my Personal Independence Payment claim as well as a questionnaire that I had to send back regarding a Work Capability Assessment for Universal Credit.

After filling in the questionnaire and posting it the same day, I read through the decision letter and couldn't understand how the assessor felt that my circumstances didn't require any support? Even though I had already found out about the decision a week earlier, as I had called to update them about my stomach pains, the decision had still shocked me!

I had decided to have the decision reviewed and explained my health further in a letter that I had sent, but it remained the same outcome, so that's when I didn't bother with it anymore.

Around this same time, I began thinking about whether I wanted to carry on with working in mental health professionally and since November 2022; I had begun to experience so many emotions, feelings, and thoughts. I kept going back and forth on my decision, so I decided to just leave it be and only focus on my health as much as I could.

If I was meant to continue working in mental health, then it would happen and if not, then I would simply step away. From understanding that I kept being severely affected by supporting others because it kept reminding me of my own trauma, I felt the right decision was to stop focusing on trying to help others when that had been my focus since I was nineteen years of age! This is because I felt it was all I was good for, as I didn't have the strength for anything else.

Now that I was thirty-one years of age and had become a grown man with so many life lessons and insights about myself and the world around me, a sacrifice needed to be made in order to finally close the past and not mention the details unless I was speaking at a specific event to raise awareness about abuse.

I could literally feel just how much I needed to take that step because the way I kept holding on and then feeling like I needed to let go, it reminded me of how I felt before I escaped and once again; I had found myself in the same scenario, so I had to remind myself of what mattered the most and that was my own happiness first.

Deep down, I think all of the signs were there from the beginning because the way I was attending groups and then needed a break and then attending them again; it wasn't who I was at all. When I had a focus in the past, nothing would take me off track, but this wasn't the case any longer.

The biggest thing that I started to do was finally accept that I may never get the outcome that I had hoped for with the help of the criminal justice system and before that happened, I needed to start letting go of the aim of getting my desired outcome, so I wouldn't be as affected once it was all over.

What I didn't realise is the more I let go of the past, the more affected I became by it and that's when all of the changes began taking place. It's like building a house where, if you're trying to place a new foundation to start something new, then you won't be able to do that unless you have demolished everything first, including the old foundation.

This is how my life felt at the time where everything that I had built on a foundation that no longer benefited me, I needed to demolish all of it and then start from the very beginning with a completely new foundation that didn't involve using any of the old foundation.

All I could do was simply follow my gut instincts and listen to my inner child as always because since I was five years of age, all I have known is abuse and seeing a specific post on Twitter allowed me to understand that walking away from mental health would be the right decision as I no longer had the emotional capacity to support others professionally that were trying to survive.

At the same time, I could feel my life pulling me away into a different direction and it was all focused around building a life where I enjoyed what I was doing without being triggered and then outside of that, I would do everything for my own self-care, self-love and happiness.

The post that I had come across was an image from a book by Michaela Angemeer that read 'if you keep trying to fix other people, it's you that's broken', and that hit me so damn hard because since the age of nineteen as I have already mentioned, all I ever tried to do was fix others when I needed to actually help fix myself!

When I say 'fix', I don't mean to mend myself where I am broken. I mean to simply help myself heal by experiencing happiness for once and living for me rather than always living for others while my life kept being held behind.

I had made it seem like I needed to take on the entire world when really, I could choose to fight for change differently because continuously speaking about the trauma and being there for others when I then couldn't be there for myself was doing me more harm than any amount of good.

I may have lost several years of my life and I may have been a completely different person to who I would have been without the abuse, but I was still that innocent boy who deserved to experience genuine happiness like any other person. For this reason, it was finally time to take back my power and become the person that I now chose to be without trying to fix others every second of my life.

It was now Tuesday 14th February 2023, and I hadn't heard back from the Metropolitan Police Force regarding the perjury and perverting the cause of justice reports, so instead of waiting further, I decided to call 101 to see what was happening.

The person that I had spoke with told me that the reports around perverting the cause of justice and perjury would need to be handled by the police officer that was investigating my complaint since the beginning of 2022 because they were linked to the failures from 2016 when I had called the police to the house, so I emailed him and received a reply the following week.

In his reply email, he stated that some complaints can't be proceeded with as it becomes sub judicial, but to leave it with him and he would see if anything could be done?

With a report from the 2007 incident that was related to perjury where I wanted to give a witness statement, the person over the phone couldn't find any reports from 2007, but something was coming up in 2008. As he wasn't certain if it was the right one, he encouraged me to request the data from the Metropolitan Police Force, so I could then be certain about what reports had been recorded on the system.

I decided to request all of my data at the same time by doing a Data Access Request from both police forces, so I could then have a full overview of everything and once that was done, it was the waiting game once again.

On Saturday 18th February 2023, I attended an event that was organised by the male survivor organisation with students from a university. The event was about Kintsugi that is a Japanese art tradition where you bring broken pieces of ceramic items back together again with gold lacquer because anything broken becomes even more beautiful.

From how severely my entire life has been left impacted by the Metropolitan Police Force, attending the event allowed me to test my social anxiety and I found that I am fully comfortable with being in the company of other survivors by knowing that I am able to be heard without even saying a word. But to travel to places and be around big crowds; I would rather be on open land alone than to feel so suffocated.

One main thing that I had hoped was my chronic insomnia didn't let me down on the day, so I made sure to make myself really tired the day before and went to bed really early, but ended up falling asleep after 11pm that was a lot better than after 2am either way.

I had set my alarm for 5:30am to continue going off every thirty minutes because I had to leave by 7:30am the latest! I was so glad when I had naturally opened my eyes at 5:10am because not only was I able to get up on time, but I was able to settle the triggers and be calm enough to travel using the public transport that I hadn't used in over a year.

From the end of February 2023 and until the end of March 2023, a few things had happened that both empowered me to keep going, and it had also left with feeling quite vulnerable that had made it feel like the end of my life was approaching me.

I had received an email informing me that the poem I had entered in the competition in October 2022 wasn't selected to be a winner. You would think that it shouldn't have affected me in any way, but that wasn't the case. This is because my poem was very personal, as it explained my journey through abuse since childhood.

Once I had processed what I was experiencing internally, I had made another big decision, and it was from viewing competitions differently. I decided that I wouldn't enter any competitions to compete with anyone because my creative work will always have a deep personal meaning and for that reason; it wasn't suitable to be competed with.

When I thought, 'what else could happen today', I had spoken too soon because the complaint that I had filed at the end of 2022 stated that both police officers had provided an acceptable service.

During the video recorded interview when two police officers had visited me, I broke down in tears when speaking about Monday 28th November 2011, the day I would have killed myself and right after, one of the police officers had stated that both of them would leave me for ten minutes? I don't know about you, but leaving someone for ten minutes after they have broken down when speaking about the day they would have killed themselves would be the last thing on my mind.

I was also given wrong information around the time limits of a crime being investigated and all of the lines of enquiries weren't followed during the criminal investigations, so if this is acceptable behaviour, then historical abuse is something that will never be taken seriously when rapists that are found guilty are being allowed to keep their freedom rather than being sent to prison!?

The biggest thing that was happening was doing the final preparation for what I had started doing since 2022. I had contacted several law firms, and I had either been told there wasn't a case, they didn't have the capacity, or I received no reply at all. I had spoken to one person, but the level of service that I should have received was so poor that I later found out they weren't even registered with the legal body of law.

After thinking over everything and understanding how severe and permanent the psychological injuries were because of the distress that had been caused by police officers from the Metropolitan Police Force, I decided to represent myself as I was going to be suing them for the losses that I had sustained!

There was something that I knew I had to do and that was to contact an independent journalist who speaks the truth about anything and everything, so my respect for her will always remain so strong.

My civil action wasn't just about being compensated for the losses, it was also about raising awareness of how severely survivors are being failed by a system that should be taking them seriously and not leaving them traumatised further. Once we had spoken via email initially and she was interested, we agreed on a date and time where I would be speaking on her Breakfast Show called Rise.

Regardless of how disappointed I may have been with the outcome of the complaint, including my poem not being a winner and the outcome of my Personal Independence Payment review, something much bigger was going to happen, so I needed to be patient for one more week as I had decided to send my Letter of Notification with a fifty-one-page document that outlined the details of my claim, including any other information that could be relevant to Sir Mark Rowley QPM, The Commissioner of the Metropolitan Police Force on the 1st April 2023.

The final nightmare that I had to put up with during that time was about my data that I had requested and since I had requested my data from the Metropolitan Police Force and when I emailed the data office for an update, they stated that my request still hadn't been assigned to someone and all they could do was apologise for not sticking to the time limit of one month while acknowledging that they had breached the Data Protection Act 2018.

The email also stated that they had been experiencing delays for a few years due to a high demand for requests, so how could they have not implemented any improvements to reduce this? The only thing that I could do was wait a further two months because usually with complex cases, three months are allowed in order to provide someone with their data.

All I had wanted since July 2019 was to address all of the abuse that I had lived through, so I could then experience closure and build a new life after, but from how the events unfolded since August 2019 once the Metropolitan Police Force had received my crime reports, it left me realising that using violence on the 24th June 2016 wouldn't have just prevented further abuse, but everything would have been addressed in a Crown Court and there is a high chance that I wouldn't have spent a single day in prison!

For this reason, I had come to the understanding that I could never trust the criminal justice system again and if anyone else or the abusers from the past tried to hurt me again, then the criminal justice system would have to tell me why they feel I should go to prison when what I may end up doing would be because they had failed me in the past and I had no faith in them helping me again!

Chapter Five

You Will Never Rewrite My Truth

The next two months that followed up until the end of May 2023, I would both be empowered and feel completely broken again as life would teach me some of the biggest lessons to help me keep growing.

The lessons that I would learn would allow me to take the steps in understanding who I really am, to accept myself as a whole and unapologetically begin putting myself first without trying to save the world in the ways I was trying to do.

It was a few weeks into April 2023 when I had spoken with an independent journalist that is a very daring truth teller and she isn't afraid of the battles she may have to experience to get the truth to the public and if you haven't already heard of her, then please allow me to introduce you to the one and only Sonia Poulton!

As I have chronic insomnia, I had hoped that I would be able to wake up early because I would be going live at 8:15am. It was a huge relief when I was able to be awake early and I didn't care about anything else that morning, apart from feeling calm and focused for the interview.

I wasn't expecting to get emotional during the interview, but you could see that I was because towards the end, I didn't hold back in expressing with such anger in my voice of why my fight for justice was so huge; to end all forms of child abuse for good!

Once the interview was over, I was experiencing all sorts of emotions, feelings and thoughts because all of the past was being triggered at the same time and it took me a few hours to fully release it all by sitting in silence and doing deep breathing exercises.

What made the journey to having my voice heard even more worthwhile was the amount of support that I received from people who had tuned in live and also the interactions on Twitter that went on for at least a week. It allowed me to understand how powerful our voices are when we finally stand up for what we believe in and people have witnessed us doing so.

I will forever be grateful to Sonia Poulton for believing in me and also giving me the opportunity to finally start being heard because, for a very long time, I felt completely silenced. Now, I had been heard publicly, and it was only just the beginning!

One thing that I had finally been able to do was to be seen by a Consultant Psychologist and I had three sessions with him. Due to chronic insomnia and his availability, the first session happened over a video call and the final two sessions took place in person.

The first session involved speaking about the past and I was glad that I didn't have to mention everything, as he had my previous reports from when I had spoken with mental health professionals. The final two sessions involved discussing the daily diary that he had asked me to keep and then completing two questionnaires that would help him understand how low or severe the C-PTSD was.

Once all three sessions were completed, I then waited a few weeks for the report and once I had received it, I read through it thoroughly while taking my time to understand everything it was saying. Should I have felt angry to finally have got a formal diagnosis that stated what I had known already for so long?

I felt a certain kind of relief by reading it because finally; I had a report to support what I had always been saying about the severity of how I had been left affected by the abusers and various police officers. For so long, I had wondered what would be possible or not after half of my life was filled with abuse and now I was aware.

I also felt comfort when I read what the Consultant Psychologist had said about any recommended medication and he didn't state any.

In fact, he stated that I had declined medication as my mental health deteriorated from how the police officers had left me affected and it was because of the closure that I never experienced.

This really hit home because the misconception about trauma is how medication is what will solve everything when, in fact, it can be because a survivor may not have experienced the closure that they have needed.

Finally, reading the recommended types of therapy brought a sense of understanding of what I could be able to handle when I felt ready because after all, I know myself better than anyone, so over the next few months, I would be able to see how I was doing in life and what type of support I may have needed.

After an entire year of trying to get a formal diagnosis, I finally had one, and it was worth every single penny because now that I had a formal diagnosis, it would allow me to have the support that I needed, it would allow me to make any further adjustments to help me keep living and finally, it would help to make life easier as I didn't need to explain everything myself when I could show the formal diagnosis.

The event that taught me some of the biggest life lessons happened at the end of April 2023. Around August 2022, if I remember correctly, I had come across a post on Twitter where a survivor had posted their journey and how they were about to start therapy.

I had commented on their post that was very heartfelt and that's how we began speaking. While having various conversations, we both shared an aspect of our healing journey that is highly misunderstood by many people both who have and haven't experienced any abuse.

From my own experiences of finding myself and healing in a similar way that isn't always spoken about openly because of the misunderstandings in society, I was able to understand them and relate directly. We had been speaking for at least a few months and then one day; the conversation took a turn that triggered me severely where I found myself in fight-or-flight mode and I felt safer to choose flight.

At the same time, I instantly realised that I felt used and the way they were speaking to me helped me to further understand that they were only interested in speaking with me for their own selfish reasons. To cut a long story short, they read what I had said and took it completely out of context because they listened to reply rather than listening to understand as they wanted to keep using me.

This then led them to verbally abusing me in a direct message before publicly posting a tweet, calling me names to maliciously attack me because they weren't happy with me wanting to step away from the conversations that we were having and ending communication with them altogether.

The way they attacked me was more than just hurtful because I had shared details about something so personal to help them understand themselves, yet there I was questioning my reality because I felt so hurt.

I couldn't understand everything so clearly at the time, but I knew how I had been impacted was on a very severe level because I wouldn't have deleted my Twitter and YouTube accounts otherwise after deciding that I didn't want to give my time to people anymore when in the end, they could hurt me after using me.

When I explained what had happened to a few people, I realised that they didn't even know my entire journey, and I had explained certain details of what had happened where they may not have understood what I was saying. At the time, I couldn't understand this because I was severely distressed, and I remained in that state for two whole months!

From this traumatic event, I understood that I didn't need to be on social media anymore if I didn't want to be. I understood that I didn't need to be seen in the way I thought I needed to be in order to make an impact that led to several changes in the world. I understood that I didn't always need to explain myself to people if they couldn't understand me to begin with and especially without knowing about my journey.

Finally, I understood that it was okay for people to view me and speak about me wrongly to others because if how they are viewing me and speaking about me isn't who I am, then they are simply misunderstood and those who end up believing the lies too quickly are too gullible and / or were already looking for a reason to hate me; even if I won't have done anything wrong.

By the end of April 2023, I had received a letter from a law firm that was representing Sir Mark Rowley QPM and it asked for information on what laws had been breached. As I had been guided by survivors, I had already become aware of how my case would be Personal Injury and the legal details related to it.

There are two laws that applied, and they were the Human Rights Act 1998 and the Data Protection Act 2018. Once I had replied to the letter, I waited a few days to receive an acknowledgement via email as that's how I sent the letter to make it quicker and save money on postage, but I hadn't received a reply email, so I called the representative at the law firm.

Finally, I had confirmation that they had received it and was aware they now had three months to investigate and then provide their Formal Response by the deadline that was the 26th July 2023.

On the 2nd June 2023, I received an email from the police officer that had been investigating my complaint into the incident that took place on the 24th June 2016 and he apologised for taking so long as he had other investigations to see to.

He also mentioned that the report would be completed within ten days, that made it feel very cathartic, as it would be a seven-year anniversary for that incident. I had also thought that he had been spoken to by the representative about the civil claim and the complaint report had then been made a priority because it was related to one of the incidents in the civil claim.

At the end of June 2023, I began wondering why the estate agent that I had complained about in 2022 hadn't got back in touch with me? Was it because they didn't care or they simply didn't receive my message?

To understand what had happened, I decided to call them and everything was resolved that very same day because it turns out that they hadn't received my message and after speaking with the Operations Manager; I came to know that the person who behaved unprofessionally had left at the end of 2022, so they weren't able to address it with him.

Instead, they were still open to understanding how they could improve, so if any of their employees would come across a similar scenario in the present or future, then they would know what to do about it.

Later that evening, I drafted up an email with a few links to different organisations that could help them with training around domestic abuse, so they weren't left wondering how they could go about making those improvements as they had the accurate support and guidance in place.

Once the email was sent and I had received acknowledgment of it being received, I finally felt heard and would look forward to hearing about the improvements that would be made as the Operations Manager had said he would keep me up to date which was very reassuring to hear.

Since the last contact that I had with the Operations Manager, I haven't received any updates, so I am unaware if anything has been implemented or not.

The day of my Work Capability Assessment had finally arrived after it had been rescheduled a few times and there was a moment where I almost felt completely silent. Thirty minutes before the assessment, I received a phone call and was made aware that the practitioner would be working from home, so the phone call wouldn't be able to be recorded.

I began wondering whether I had written down in the form of wanting the assessment recorded and I then remembered that I had because I was going to use it as evidence within the civil claim. However, not having the phone call recorded wasn't essential in the end because I would be able to request the report once the decision had been made and that would be as good as the phone call.

If I had stated that I still wanted to have the phone call recorded, then that would have meant the assessment being rescheduled once again and I would most likely have had to wait another month! There was no way I was willing to wait another month again, so I told them it was okay if the phone call wasn't recorded and, thankfully, there were no other moments of panic.

The assessment lasted around two hours and I had stated everything that I was asked. It brought back every trauma that I had experienced and describing how I was left feeling by the Metropolitan Police Force just brought an insane amount of anger. From the things that I had mentioned about suicide ideation and how vulnerable I was feeling in that moment, the practitioner had a duty to inform someone.

They were going to inform the crisis team, but because I stated that speaking to them would only trigger me more, they suggested calling my doctor and I was okay with that. About an hour later, I received a phone call from my doctor and explained everything that he needed to know.

From how concerned he became, I gave him permission to refer me to a psychiatrist, so at least he could sleep at night and not worry about me. In that moment, I was certain that therapy wasn't going to help me because I needed closure and not speaking about how I was feeling, but I also knew that the pain could become bearable within a few months if I had experienced closure by then, so there was no harm in being referred either way.

All I knew was I needed a miracle because I didn't have a single clue about what I could do to experience closure and I needed closure, desperately! The scenario that allowed me to understand just how desperately I needed closure was when I could no longer cry, even while being completely intoxicated on alcohol.

From being able to cry whilst drunk and then not being able to cry at all made me feel severely suffocated to the point my chest pains became slightly worse. To not be able to release the pain through my tears where it continues to be held in, it's worse than death itself.

In fact, I no longer wanted to be within my body anymore because I didn't see the point in staying alive if the pain would continue getting worse and there was nothing that would be able to stop it, so I had made a decision and depending on what would happen over the next few months or even an entire year until the civil claim was fully over, I would either still be alive or finally resting in peace.

A few days before the Work Capability Assessment, I hadn't heard back from the police officer that was still investigating the complaint, so I decided to email him. Let's just say that I would still be waiting for an update because even though he replied, he didn't give me any new updates on whether he had completed the report or not!? Instead, he simply stated that he had just come back from leave and he would go back on leave the following day, so he would update me in August!?

I didn't know what to say while feeling really let down and what made it worse was the reply that I had got from the Metropolitan Police Force's Data Office.

I had emailed for an update as I hadn't heard anything for a month since a caseworker had been assigned to my request after I had filed a complaint once three months had been reached and in that moment; I was finding out that a new caseworker had been assigned without me being informed?

I replied back kindly asking them to update me about every small change that happens because from how I was left feeling by various police officers; I had C-PTSD and for that reason, anything that happened without me being informed would affect me severely.

How many more times would I be let down by professionals who aren't able to do the smallest of things!? To update someone via email of a new caseworker being assigned doesn't take that long at all when writing the email only takes a few minutes at the most.

My life had reached a point where I was so tired of having everything addressed that I was finally ready to let it all go once the civil claim was fully over.

From simply wanting to have the abusers prosecuted for how they abused me, the life that I was building after already being abused for twenty years had been completely destroyed.

The most traumatising truth that I began finding impossible to live with is if the police officers had actually cared and did what they were supposed to do, then the abusers would have successfully been prosecuted.

This is because even though there may not have been either any or enough evidence for the child sexual abuse, domestic abuse and any other reports that I had filed, there was enough evidence to show they had lied and that itself is a crime that carries a life sentence!

During mid-July 2023, I could feel myself becoming impatient because the deadline for me to receive the Formal Response was slowly approaching. Each day felt like an entire week, and I just hoped the final few days didn't become severely unbearable.

At the same time, I also wondered whether I would actually receive it by the 26th July 2023 or not? Would I have to write a letter stating the deadline had passed and if so, how long would they take to reply to it? When they finally would reply, what would they say and would they state they accepted liability or deny it? If they denied it, then what would my reaction and next steps be?

Wednesday 26th July 2023 had finally arrived, and I remained anxious for the entire day. I found myself looking at the clock every few minutes until I decided to lie down and rest while trying to shut off my mind by watching a comedy. It helped a little, but I still found myself looking at the clock.

Once the day had reached 5pm, I had no other option but to accept that the deadline had been missed! Rather than driving myself into an emotional mess, I decided to wait until Monday just in case they had sent it in the post and there was a problem with the service.

Over the weekend, I had drafted a letter that I would send to the representative after 11am on Monday morning, as that's usually when the post would arrive by.

During the late morning on Monday, I read over the letter that I had drafted before printing it off, signing it and sending it off via First Class Post with a copy of the letter also sent via email before waiting to hear back.

I had already decided that if I didn't hear back by the 11th August 2023, that was the extended deadline that I had given, then I would call the representative the following week to see if I could get a response that way. Thankfully, I didn't need to do that because on Monday 7th August 2023; I received an email from him.

The email asked me to accept their apologies with an explanation of why they had missed the deadline because in the letter that I had sent; I had asked for both their formal response to state whether they accepted or denied liability and an explanation of what caused the deadline to be missed?

The reason was they were very busy or away, but that wasn't a good enough reason to not have informed me even a day prior to the 26th July 2023 explaining they wouldn't be able to stick to the deadline and if it was okay to have an extension for a few weeks?

They had also confirmed receiving my letter both via email and post after I had asked in a follow-up email because the postage tracking didn't show a confirmation, so I decided to report the issue to Royal Mail.

Finally, the email asked whether they could have an extension for another week by 4pm on 18th August 2023 to give me their Formal Response. I decided to give it to them as it was only by a week and they had made it feel like it was a certainty of me receiving it by then.

Friday 18th August 20023 had finally arrived and a few minutes before 3pm, I received an email, but it didn't include a Formal Response.

It simply explained that because the representative hadn't received some documents from his client and as the complaint outcome report regarding the incident on the 24th June 2016 was still ongoing, they wouldn't be able to provide a Formal Response until the outcome report had been finalised.

After exchanging a few emails with the representative and the police officer that was investigating the complaint, it was agreed that I would receive a Formal Response within twenty-eight days of the complaint outcome report being completed and because I didn't know when that would be; I didn't give another deadline.

You may wonder why I didn't start legal proceedings during this time and it's because I already knew that the case would be put on hold while the same thing happened of receiving the complaint outcome report and the Formal Response. The case wasn't ready to be heard in the High Court and it would involve unnecessary stress, so the easier thing was to simply wait.

The three-year deadline for me to start legal proceedings would be the 25th April 2025, so I still had a long way to go that gave me the safety of trying to have the civil claim addressed out of court first as that's what is usually required because legal proceedings is considered as the final step where you have no other way of addressing a civil claim.

And if and when I would start legal proceedings, the High Court would come to know that Sir Mark Rowley QPM hadn't stuck to the deadlines that not only caused me further distress, but more inconvenience and they could be liable to pay extra costs, so for me there wasn't any rush in having it settled when I already knew that whatever would happen, my truth wouldn't let me down when it has always helped me through.

The day had finally arrived for me to make an adjustment to my life that I never thought I would ever have to experience and the moment my eyes had opened around 4am; I wasn't going to allow myself to close them by knowing that I could fall into a deep sleep and not be able to wake up even with the alarms that I had set.

As the vasectomy was going to be happening under general anesthetic, I didn't have to worry about not eating and drinking anything in the morning, but at the same time, my self-awareness was spinning out of control as I didn't know how I would be impacted emotionally while it was happening.

The admission time was 7am, so I needed to be on time without any delay, but there was a moment that made me panic and the rain that morning wasn't pleasant either. While I was travelling on the bus, I kept wondering when it would be my stop and usually the bus would read out the names of the stops, but it stopped doing that and as it was still dark outside, I couldn't see much.

It was like that scene in a movie where the character looks out of the window and the look of complete disbelief is printed all over their face at what they have just seen. That's what my reaction was like when I saw the bus stop I was meant to get off at had passed! Immediately, I stood up and pressed the stop button before getting off at the next stop.

It took me around ten minutes to walk back and all I kept hoping was nothing else would almost go wrong that day. Once I had finally arrived at the hospital, I followed the signs and found the ward that I would be in for the next few hours before being shown to my bed where another gentleman was already waiting at his bed before two other gentlemen joined us in the same room.

I was told by the nurse that was taking care of me that the vasectomy would take place after 10am and the surgeon would come down to speak with me before that, so there were a few hours of waiting around.

All I could think was, "why does my life have to be this traumatic? I simply wanted to live my life since I was sixteen years of age and now at thirty-one years of age, I am having to make an adjustment and sacrificing my right to become a father because the Metropolitan Police Force thought it was okay to leave me feeling like I was a nobody. How is any of this fair when the abusers have been living their lives even while abusing me and mine has remained non-existent since the age of five!?"

Later that morning and after I had spoken to the surgeon, I got changed into my dressing gown and slippers before waiting to be taken to the surgery room and that's when it fully hit me of the reality because before that day, my mental health could have felt better where I didn't have to go through with the vasectomy.

While walking to the surgery room and once I had finally laid on the bed, my reality had been fully confirmed and the permanent psychological injuries would remain for the rest of my life!

As the vasectomy was taking place, I was speaking to the nurses and surgeons just to make conversation and before I was rolled into the main surgery room on the bed; I had explained to one of the nurses that I would tell everyone why I may cry before it began, so if I ended up crying, then there was an understanding of how major it was for me to have the vasectomy.

After making some conversation, it slowly led me to explain why I had to go through with it and that's when I cried because the emotional pain was so unbearable! Two of the nurses continued wiping away my tears as I laid there explaining how the Metropolitan Police Force had left me feeling as the surgeon was informing me of everything that was happening.

Once he had mentioned that both of my tubes were cut, something changed within me and until I got home later that day, I was too traumatised to understand it thoroughly. A few more minutes later and I was back in the ward having some tea and toast as I wiped the rest of my tears while trying not to cry again because I didn't feel safe to do so from how vulnerable I had felt already.

After I had been given the paperwork and a sample bottle, I was able to go home and the moment I stepped through the door; it had finally hit me! It felt like an out-of-body experience where I was taken right back to the surgery room and could see everything that had happened.

I could see myself laying on the bed crying while the nurses were wiping away my tears as the surgery was being carried out and I then saw myself standing next to a woman who would have been my wife where she was giving birth to our child. I could then see myself laying back down and it felt like I had just killed my children. It felt like I was seeing a glimpse of my future that had been completely taken from me and that's something that I still find unbearable to process.

As I was writing this almost two months later, I realised that I set myself and my unborn children free by completely killing all of the connections to the abusers because it ends with me!

A few weeks later, I received two emails that informed me I had a message to read and something to do on my Universal Credit account and let's just say that for the next three weeks, my existence was hanging by a thread! My payment had been suspended and there was a message from The Risk Review Team that stated I wasn't entitled to Universal Credit because of doubts about the legitimacy of my claim?

To say that I was left confused is an understatement and once I had finally spoken to someone the following day after leaving two messages in my journal explaining how my mental health had been impacted from what had just begun, I was required to provide several documents.

In the end, there were between fifty to a hundred documents that I had provided and it included pictures of me head to toe standing outside of the house, then outside of my flat door and so on. It was only after a week had gone by where I felt slightly calm enough to do a search online that allowed me to understand what had happened because the lady who was in charge of investigating my claim had told me that she wasn't allowed to give me any details at all.

How can my life have been investigated that was a completely degrading treatment, yet I wasn't allowed to know any details apart from being told they were verifying my claim to make sure that I was receiving the right amount of Universal Credit!? What I experienced was a benefit fraud investigation and it wasn't because I had done anything wrong.

During the pandemic in 2020, the DWP had dropped all procedures to do identity checks and just accepted everyone onto Universal Credit that fit the criteria. Scammers had got together where several fraudulent Universal Credit claims had been made and because of that, The Risk Review Team were put together to verify every claim that was flagged as high-risk fraud.

Once the investigation was finally over and I had proven my claim was legitimate, I contacted an organisation who were actively fighting against such treatment because if sharing my experience with them can help their fight to address the severity of it, then that's all that mattered.

I also filed a complaint with the DWP in the hope that they gave me a full explanation while accepting how insensitive their process was and for that to change. Once I had received a phone call a few days after filing the complaint, it was confirmed that the cyber surveillance team had flagged my name and the reason may not have been about my claim specifically as it could have been the area I was living in, someone using my identity and so on, but I wasn't allowed to be given any other specific details about it and if they were to look into things further, then any specific details would only remain with them.

I don't understand how a person's life can be investigated, yet they aren't able to know every detail about it when sharing those details wouldn't involve any specific details about how organisations investigate people?

Nevertheless, I had stated everything that I needed to, including the improvements that should be made, so hopefully no other genuine person experiences the extreme treatment that I had to go through.

During this entire madness, I had finally received an email on the 5th October 2023 from the police officer that was investigating the complaint regarding the incident on the 24th June 2016 and he stated that the complaint report was completed which would then go through the Quality Assurance Process before it would be sent to me.

A few more months and I hoped that I would finally have the Formal Response that would then help me to decide on the next steps of my civil claim against the Metropolitan Police Force.

It was now the end of December 2023 and when I thought my life couldn't get any worse; I was wrong. Since the complaint report had entered the Quality Assurance Process, I had emailed the investigating officer a few times to ask for his help in getting an update from the police officer on how long it would take until the report would be sent to me?

I had also asked him to pass on the message of it being a priority if he wasn't aware about it already and he had confirmed that the Professional Standards Unit had contacted him to enquire about the complaint report being a priority and he had chased for it as he knew how important it was for me to have it. But in the emails that followed after that, no reply had been received by me.

The complete silence and lack of updates took me right back to when the whole nightmare with the Metropolitan Police Force had begun in August 2019 and because I experienced a similar service from August 2019, my mental health had finally hit breaking point.

I felt the same way as how I felt a few months before Monday 28th November 2011, where I was left suicidal and felt that it was the end of my life. What made it worse this time is so much more abuse had been experienced by me and as I didn't have much of a life to look forward to already, it made it impossible to find a strong enough reason to want to continue living.

I remained completely petrified, and I didn't tell anyone just how severe my mental health had deteriorated because I didn't want anyone to worry about it. I also didn't want the help this time because speaking about it would only trigger me more by having to remember what my reality was like while also being aware of what I had already accepted a few months ago; if my life is meant to end this time, then I won't stop it from happening.

By the end of December 2023, The Metropolitan Police Force had taken me right back to 2011 when my journey to finding the truth had begun, except this time, it was about a journey of knowing everything and trying to have the closure that I needed. Would I be speaking while still breathing or would it be my message through a suicide note; the following year would show me!

What brought the year to a close was reflecting over four different things that had also happened. The first thing was hearing back from the organisation that I had contacted regarding my experience of being investigated during the fraud investigation with the DWP.

They had spoken to a law firm that was thinking about using my case study to push for a Judicial Review and I would find out after the New Year as they hadn't decided due to being busy with several other cases.

The second thing that I reflected over was doing a podcast with a lady called Karen that had interviewed me at the start of the year about my experiences with stalking.

Just how the conversation flowed the first time I spoke with Karen, the conversation flowed once again during the podcast and even though we had prepared enough to make it feel natural for the audience like we were having a conversation rather than an interview, the final version that I had listened to left me blown away because it turned out so well!

All of the messages that I had wanted to share during the podcast had been shared and everything that I wanted to say about the various questions had been said.

In fact, while I was writing this, I don't think that I found myself going over the podcast in my head after it was done and telling myself things like, 'I could have said this or I could have said that in another way'. I was left truly speechless because for the first time, I had said everything that needed to be said and in a way that I was completely happy with.

The third thing that I reflected over was taking part in a male peer support group that went on for eight weeks with the male survivor organisation and the experience was completely soul cleansing! I learnt so much about myself as a male survivor and by listening to other male survivors who had coped in similar ways, it finally allowed me to feel heard once again!

I had felt alone in a way because even though I had spoken to male survivors previously, the actual details themselves of the journey after abuse wasn't discussed much. This helped me to process several things and understand so many aspects of my own healing journey. Without realising it, it was something that I deeply needed and I am so glad that I decided to take part.

The fourth and final thing that I reflected over was a new movement that I had started for social change and it happened so naturally without me even having to try to create something.

The way it came about was by taking part in a distant Reiki Healing with a Spiritual Soul named Zoë and she has a YouTube Channel called Synchronised Souls Podcast. The experience was so powerful and what I experienced during the healing and after is something that I am still trying to understand because of the new light for life that I had started to see.

It feels like it removed several emotional blocks that had been preventing me from being able to enjoy my creative side and finally, I no longer felt held back!

The movement that I started is called Healing The Silence, and it simply means to heal the various aspects of the trauma that no one else can understand apart from the person that has experienced it themselves.

As I could no longer work, this new energy that I had found to continue healing through Art Therapy is what allowed me to understand that I could still have a future and the main goal would be to become an International Public Speaker just like I had planned since 2016. At the same time, I kept an open mind because life ends up surprising us when we least expect it, so I could find myself doing something completely different! Either way, I remained very curious and couldn't wait to find out!

The New Year had begun and as I still hadn't heard back from the police officer that was carrying out the Quality Assurance Process for the complaint report, I decided to send a letter to Sir Mark Rowley QPM's representative. The five pages covered every aspect of how the delay in receiving the complaint report and their Formal Response could have been avoided, but more importantly, it gave a third and final extended deadline.

I had reached a point where my mental health could no longer cope with any further distress and it became a very uncertain time of not knowing how I would react to the way I was feeling each day.

The following day, I received an email from the representative and they stated that they would find out what was happening with the complaint report and then get back to me very soon.

They also explained that they had received my previous communications via email, but were intending to reply to it when they provided their Formal Response. I replied back and stated that I would await their email regarding the complaint report and also understood what they had said about my previous communications, while expressing that receiving a quick acknowledgement would have been preferred.

Even though I was hoping that they would get back to me and provide me with the relevant documents by the third and final extended deadline, a part of me wondered whether I actually would hear back. This one thought allowed me to start preparing myself for the final step and that was legal proceedings.

I waited no further and started getting all of the documents ready that I would need to send to the High Court and the representative, so if and when that time had arrived, I wouldn't have to start stressing myself out because everything would already be prepared. The only thing that I would need to do is include the date and my signature on various documents.

As I had already started preparing a few documents from the end of August 2023, I didn't need to do much to start getting prepared, so I had already made life easier for me once 2024 had begun. The only thing that would determine what would be happening over the next few months is whether I would have both the complaint outcome report and the Formal Response by Friday 29th March 2024 by 5pm or not?

On Wednesday 17th January 2024, I had received the complaint report and my entire body was instantly filled with anxiety! I felt so confident in thinking that it would state what I hoped it would and I felt so focused on viewing the event from the way that it had happened with the truth, but what I didn't think about was how the report could have been recorded on the system and how the report could be so inaccurate of what really happened.

This was the reality that I was faced with because several details were inaccurate of what really happened on the day and after. I couldn't understand how what I had said wasn't included in the report, but after a few days had passed, I came to a conclusion that had made sense.

After I had been told to go for a walk to cool down, the police officers may have spoken to the parents alone and the lies that they would have told them is what was included in the system because there were details of false reasons for why the incident had occurred that I hadn't mentioned myself because they weren't the actual reasons.

Over the next few weeks, I had sent a few letters to the representative explaining all of the inaccurate details to help him and Sir Mark Rowley QPM become aware of what really happened, so they had all of the accurate information that they would need to decide whether they would be accepting liability in full / part or denying it completely?

I had continued to keep organising all of the documents and printing off the ones that I needed if I would be starting legal proceedings and after looking at the complaint report again; I felt like I needed to have it reviewed from how inaccurate the details were, that kept me very unhappy with it.

Without waiting any further, I phoned the representative, and we spoke for an hour, where it became clear that he and Sir Mark Rowley QPM had thought the civil claim was for two different claims rather than it being a whole claim.

I also explained further details to help him understand why that was the case and by the end of the conversation, we both had an understanding that as the 24th June 2016 incident had laid a foundation for the permeant psychological injuries to be sustained from the events that unfolded from August 2019 rather than it being a separate scenario, having the complaint report reviewed wouldn't put the civil claim on hold and I was so glad to hear that!

As I had received the complaint report before the end of February 2024, the deadline for me to receive the Formal Response was now Wednesday 14th February 2024 by 4pm.

On Sunday 11th February 2024, I had received an email from the representative and they had asked for me to send the C-PTSD diagnosis, so I sent nine different documents that were relevant to the diagnosis including the diagnosis report itself and that way all of the documents could to be looked over at the same time in order to understand every aspect of the injuries.

When I had read over the Pre-Action Procedures and Protocols for a Personal Injury civil claim, I kept thinking that medical reports would only be exchanged after I had received a Formal Response that stated liability was admitted in part or full, but because I wasn't certain about this and as I didn't have a solicitor, even though I had tried for the second time at the beginning of February 2024, I didn't have any details to confirm the questions that I had.

The only thing that I could do was to keep going by knowing that my truth would always remain the same because it is stated on several documents, so if Sir Mark Rowley QPM wasn't following the rules, then it wouldn't make much of a difference to me when the truth is what would always stay above any unfairness.

As the deadline for me to receive the Formal Response was only three days away, I remained very anxious and the only way I could shut off my mind was to cope the way I had been coping since 2022 and that was by getting drunk several times a week whereas before 2024, it would only be a maximum of three times every two weeks.

Wednesday 14th February 2024 had arrived and when I thought that I couldn't be more anxious than I had already been for the last three days, I was wrong! My thoughts were all over the place and my emotions were doing cartwheels like they had never done them before because finally, I was going to have the Formal Response!

It was around 3:30pm when I sent the representative an email to see if an email had been sent and I hadn't received it, or would I still be receiving it by 4pm? Once 4pm had arrived and no email had been received, the deadline had been missed again!

I felt so let down and couldn't quite believe my reality because all I had experienced was several delays and this time, there was no excuse for not meeting the deadline! It was around an hour and ten minutes when I received an email with the Formal Response and some other documents.

After reading the Formal Response, I replied to the email and corrected a few things that weren't accurate before stating that I was closing the civil claim down because not only was liability fully denied, but from how it was written, it was clear that whatever had happened; I had no chances of being successful in winning the entire claim if I had decided to take it to the High Court.

Even though there was an aspect of the claim that I could have won, the rest of the incidents wouldn't have brought an outcome because of several scenarios that all played against me and as I wouldn't achieve what I had originally set out to achieve as a whole, legal proceedings was out of the question, even though Sir Mark Rowley QPM had missed the deadline for the third time!

I had explained everything in full detail within several documents over several months and somehow, it still wasn't enough to understand what I had said. I was already aware that if a civil claim isn't able to be understood on what is being claimed, then it would be struck out without any hearing taking place, so I already knew the tactics that were being played.

As the call record transcript was no longer available for the incident on the 24th June 2016 when I had to call the police, it was clear that my truth would remain a scenario where it was my words against the police officers.

The civil claim was about being compensated for the losses that had occurred from the distress that had been caused by several police officers, including addressing child abuse and raising awareness to prevent such failures from happening to others, but as I wasn't going to achieve this in the way that I needed to experience it, I had to make the impossible decision of finally walking away.

From the reality that I was now faced with, I closed the requests to have my records being sent to me and having the complaint reviewed for the 24th June 2016 incident before self-referring to talking therapy with the male survivor organisation that I was already supporting.

I had also contacted the Criminal Injuries Compensation Authority to provide some supporting documents to see if they could compensate me for the losses of income and pension contributions because even though I had to leave the apprenticeship after being further distressed by a police officer, the trauma that was re-triggered is related to the abuse itself.

Finally, all of the paper and digital copies of the documents that I no longer needed were destroyed because rather than keeping them when I would never need them again and causing myself more distress by reading over them several times that would have led to me being found dead, I needed to finally let go and accept that no one would ever be held accountable.

When I think about the entire journey since starting the civil claim on the 1st April 2023, I went to the very end of a survivor's journey to the point that there was literally nothing else left to do. Even though I didn't start legal proceedings or sue the abusers after knowing it wasn't going to allow me to feel heard and be seen in the ways that I needed to experience it, I had crossed every other path to try to have the closure that I needed.

For this reason, there will never come a time where I will look back and regret not crossing a certain path and at the same time, I have gained the knowledge to help guide other victims, survivors, advocates and allies on their own journey, so they can start living their lives a lot sooner after getting all of the help that they may need.

This is something that I was finally ready for myself and it was to address everything in therapy that had happened since July 2022 before starting to build a new life as best as I could.

Even though I had decided not to have any therapy again by knowing that it would only anger me, I wanted to give life one more chance because I wanted to see what my future had in store for me. After all, I must have been born for a reason to live through such abuse and still be alive, right?

As the end had finally arrived in looking for answers and trying to address the past in order to have the closure that I had always needed, the time had come to close this chapter of my life for good by knowing that this ending would allow me to start a new beginning!

Chapter Six

The Detox Begins

Imagine you have been working in a certain role that has involved inhaling toxic fumes each day and no matter what you have tried to do to safeguard yourself, your health has still been impacted so severely that you only realise the severity of it when you have been away from the toxic environment for a while.

Your mind and body have become so exhausted that it doesn't know how to function anymore and when you think that you're slowly beginning to feel better, your health gets worse that leaves you feeling completely lifeless; have you ever felt this way before?

It had been almost two months since receiving the Formal Response and so much had happened because I did what I have always known to do in order to help myself feel better and that's to keep going because if I had decided to remain still, then I would have fallen.

It's sort of like having to keep running so you can jump to safety from the holes in the ground that you may come across and if you were to slow down even a little, then you wouldn't have the height that would be needed in the jump to safely land on solid ground.

For the first time in my entire life, I wasn't addressing anything that was related to the past apart from my mental health and one would think that I would be resting after fighting such a battle since I was only five years of age after being abused for the first time, but I didn't know how to rest completely because all I have ever known is to keep my mind distracted from the reality that has felt impossible to live with.

One of the biggest things that had happened was giving the 1st April 2024 a closure, and I achieved this by producing a film that is called 'In Death Comes Freedom' which I then uploaded to my YouTube channel @HealingTheSilence.

Originally, it was meant to be a shadow puppetry video that explained my journey during the civil action, but when I got to the step of sketching out drawings to then cut out the templates, it felt like my message was meant to be something more?

I thought about several creative methods before giving myself some time to shut off from it and, in its own way, it would turn into whatever it was meant to become. Sometimes, we need the space for the ideas to be digested rather than trying to eat so much more that then leads to making ourselves feel sick.

It had been at least two weeks when I was certain about the new idea that was formed because the storyline wasn't meant to be about just explaining the journey during the civil action. It was meant to be about showing a very raw portrayal of what injustice can lead to.

From filming scenes that involved showing myself while speaking and then a transition into text with some background music, the storyline became the outcome that would have happened if I hadn't helped myself to stay alive once again.

During the entire process of writing, producing and editing the film that was meant to be a short film, so many emotions, feelings and thoughts were experienced because I understood that the world needed to see a survivor's struggle as they usually only hear about it.

The struggle wasn't just about getting out of bed but the process of leaving this world for good because this time around; I didn't have anything to live for, as it had all been destroyed by the Metropolitan Police Force. As I struggled to understand how I could experience the closure that was meant to happen through the civil action, which was no longer my reality, I felt that closure would never be experienced in any other way.

In order for the film to be what it had become as the outcome, I experienced two major light-bulb moments and this was during the talking therapy sessions as I was slowly processing all of the events that had occurred since July 2022.

For several years, I had always believed that closure could only be experienced when those that have harmed you and failed you are held accountable for their actions. This is because it's how society has encouraged us to live our lives where justice can only be served within a courtroom, and if those that have harmed and failed us haven't been found guilty and sent to prison or lost their position in power, then that must mean they are innocent?

The reality is, just because a person is found guilty doesn't mean that they are truly guilty and those that are found innocent, it doesn't mean that they are truly innocent because in the world that we are living in today; we hear more about injustice than justice.

When I started reflecting over every step that I had taken since I was a child and all of the things that I had learned about justice and healing / recovery, I was left wondering whether I still had the same mindset as April 2023 when I had started the civil claim.

In a way, I shouldn't have been as speechless as I had become from understanding that my entire mindset was completely different because as we grow through experiences, we won't always see things in the same ways as we once did or remain the same person as we once may have been.

However, being left completely speechless makes a lot of sense because from the light-bulb moments that I experienced, not only did I start becoming a new person, but I saw justice and healing / recovery in a way that allowed me to start experiencing small amounts of closure without even trying.

It was one of those moments where you are just getting on with the day while coping with the crisis that you may find yourself in and the cry for help that you may have cried several times, it's finally answered and you realise that you have always had the control over speaking your truth that doesn't need to be spoken in a courtroom in order to experience the justice that you have always had the right to receive as your birthright in this world.

The main scenario that allowed this light-bulb moment to be experienced was accepting that so much more harm had been caused through every legal battle that I had faced and from being left permanently psychologically damaged in certain ways by the criminal justice system itself, no amount of years in prison for the abusers, revenge or money to compensate me will ever be enough to make up for the pain that is left as the pain can never be replaced!

Once I had started accepting this impossible truth without fighting it any longer, including that those who harmed me and failed me will always remain free to live their lives without any consequences for their words and actions towards me, I was left with a new meaning of what justice now means to me which will remain until my death because I can never have any faith or trust in the criminal justice system again!

My new meaning of justice has a very specific message behind it which is, "I will speak my truth however I decide to go about it without being afraid of the consequences that I may have to face because if I had used violence than ever trusting the criminal justice system, then not only would my case have been heard in a courtroom, not only would I have been experiencing life in all aspects, but I would have never been left with the permanent psychological injuries that I will now be processing for the rest of my life.

Take yourself back to a time where you felt powerless and then something may have happened, such as coming across some information that allowed you to feel even more powerful than you may have already been feeling.

This is how I felt and it's why the film that I produced needed to be told in the way I wrote the storyline because the system no longer holds the right to have a say in my life when their time is over, and for this reason, I refused to allow them to harm me any further!

Even though I started to gain back my power by experiencing these light-bulb moments, I still felt severely distressed because having to accept the impossible reality isn't something that can be achieved over a few months, and even though I no longer had a plan in place to end my life, it was still early days because the emotional pain that I was experiencing on a daily basis continued to keep me in a very dark place.

It was a week before the film went live when I was having a shower and was left feeling so helpless because it felt like I was taken all the way back to November 2011 when my journey to finding the truth had fully begun after deciding to get the help that I needed than to end my life. It felt like I was back within the mindset that I was in and I was now having to start all over again.

I also thought about all of the personal and professional achievements that I had experienced since November 2011 to April 2024 and couldn't help but feel so broken when I realised that the life I had safeguarded to experience even after being abused for twenty years, it had been completely destroyed from the distress that had been caused during the entire legal battle between August 2019 to February 2024, but, realistically; it had begun on the 24th June 2016.

I found it unbearable to think about where I could have been in life within this time frame because if my experiences with the Metropolitan Police Force hadn't been so destructive, then I would have been experiencing life in every aspect and those that had harmed me would have been in prison, even though it might have been only for a few years.

The emotional pain that I experienced during this realisation had me feeling so helpless that I wanted to cry my eyes out, but it wasn't possible any longer because of the Metropolitan Police Force! How could this much injustice ever be okay for any human to live with!?

Even as I was writing this, the amount of emotional and psychological pain that I was experiencing was enough to want to end my life, and I have had that thought for several years. I sometimes wonder why shouldn't I just end my life because it has only become more traumatised than ever being any easier.

I then think about that moment in August 2016 when I experienced the epiphany, and I saw myself standing next to God who showed me how much pain I would live through if I chose this life, but in the end, so many major changes would be achieved for humanity. Could this have simply been wishful thinking during a time where I felt so helpless or could this actually be the truth?

Just how I stepped away from every belief in 2011, I started experiencing the same thing and once again during a time where I felt so helpless; I realised the biggest truth about the 24th June 2016 incident and from the eruptive anger that I experienced; I was left feeling in a very alarmed state that lasted for a few days.

It felt like someone had played a short scene in my head and I saw a sentence that gave me the understanding of knowing the Metropolitan Police Force had exposed themselves that proves the 24th June 2016 incident was covered up from the lies that they had told within the complaint outcome report and their Formal Response!

I began wondering whether I should have started legal proceedings while coming to terms with the truth that I now had understood, but after a few weeks had gone by, I knew that starting legal proceedings wouldn't have been enough because being compensated for the injuries wouldn't have changed the injustices that had already occurred. For this reason, criminal investigations and prosecutions against several police officers with me being compensated also is what would now be enough. Furthermore, prosecutions against the abusers also will set off the fireworks!

After processing everything for a few weeks and talking through everything with my therapist, it led to doing something that I had constantly thought about since stepping away from the civil claim and that was to write a letter to the High Court. What I couldn't understand even during March 2024 is what to write in the letter and what was the actual aim for it?

The scenario that my therapist and I had initially discussed was the fight that I couldn't let go of because I had been looking for answers and trying to address everything since I was a child, so it was my normal life and moving away from it felt uncomfortable. For this reason, I was trying to do things that kept me living within that comfortable reality that had been created by those that had abused me and failed me.

This made complete sense at the time because it really was my reality, but I then thought about how I felt and that's where the real reason had risen to the surface because it was covered with thousands of pieces that blinded me from being able to see the real truth; writing this letter was the final step to ending this battle, regardless of the outcome.

It had occurred twice where I deleted the letter that I had started writing because it felt like I was just repeating myself all over again that wasn't my aim and if that's all I wanted to do, then I would have gone through the trouble of requesting the documents that I had already written and sent those to the High Court instead.

The way I had written the letter in the end had allowed me to say what I needed to say by allowing someone who would be reading it to place themselves within my shoes even for that moment to help them understand the journey that I had faced since the 24th June 2016 and how my entire life had been left impacted by April 2024.

Once the letter had been written, I gave it a few days and then did a final read before adding a bit more that brought it to twenty pages. I was happy with how it had turned out and everything that I needed to say had been said while also understanding that once you have been away emotionally and psychologically from something that has caused you severe distress, the time you come back to it will allow you to experience just how unbearable it truly was.

This left me wondering how I was able to fight through that entire legal battle and how I was still alive because realistically, the amount of distress that I had experienced while writing the letter was more than anyone could handle, so to keep going for almost five years since August 2019, anger and the fight to be heard and to be seen is what kept pushing me, until I could no longer take any further victim blaming and gaslighting.

When the letter had been received by the High Court, I was able to finally start moving my focus onto more positive things to help myself get better and start building a new life because it truly was the end. However, this could end up changing if I received a reply that explained my entire case would be heard and not just certain aspects of it. I had described everything that had happened, including the lies that expose the Metropolitan Police Force for being fully accountable, so if the High Court agreed, then that's the only time I would start legal proceedings.

This is because there is a law in place that gives complete immunity to police officers from facing any liability of negligence during criminal investigations, so I needed to be certain about where I stood which wasn't possible by trying to have legal advice because even when I was willing to pay for it, a law firm simply wished me the best in finding it from someone else after looking through all of the documents.

This is how much injustice is happening where police officers that don't care about providing an efficient service are getting away with causing such psychological harm to the people they're supposed to serve! How can this law even be in place because the Victims' Code of Practices guides every police officer on what they need to do when coming in contact with every victim?

I don't know if this is for certain but when I was doing some research into this law and I came across a specific case that was heard in the High Court, it may have stated that the law was put into place, so police officers didn't feel afraid in doing their job by thinking that they could be held liable for negligence.

By reading the Victims' Code of Practices myself, if everything that is stated in there had been followed by the four police officers on the 24th June 2016, then I would have received the highest level of service and that's when my life would have changed for the better without any further abuse being experienced because I would have been saved!

Even though I was severely failed, if the Victims' Code of Practices had been followed from August 2019, then I wouldn't have experienced such an extremely poor service once again, so the law that gives police officers complete immunity from negligence during criminal investigations, it doesn't make any sense for it to be in place when it allows police forces to get away with so much injustice while leaving victims, survivors, and allies screaming to be heard and to be seen! When you are doing everything that you are supposed to do, there is no room for failures and failures only occur when every step hasn't been taken that should have been taken.

As you may now be able to see this scenario a lot more clearly, it's why the letter needed to be written to the High Court because I needed to first bring it to their attention of just how major my case is for the public interest, but also to explain that if my case couldn't be heard in its entirety, then the letter could be kept as a record to then be used as evidence if it was ever needed regarding any cases that may arise which were related to the truth that I would always continue speaking publicly.

After all, if the Metropolitan Police Force have stated that no crime was reported by anyone on the 24th June 2016, if I was told on the day that it wouldn't go any further, then why would there have been ongoing contact after the incident which is what they had also stated as their version of events in reply to my claim?

This is the truth that I understood that exposes them because it doesn't make any sense and if specialists who aren't biased were to analyse every record that is relevant to the 24th June 2016 and after, then it would only prove what I have always known, I was completely failed and the Metropolitan Police Force then lied while taking every single step that they could to fabricate my truth that also involved destroying evidence that proved a crime had been reported by me!

While processing my new reality and having to accept it no matter how unbearable the emotional and psychological pain had become, I started to focus on my mental health while trying to put my happiness first, for once, when I had always been surrounded by negativity. The only way I was able to keep my focus on looking forward to the future was by keeping myself focused on what I enjoyed doing and this is when I started to get back into the hobbies that I once loved, but this wasn't so easy as first because I had to start enjoying them again from losing complete interest throughout the years.

I knew that some hobbies wouldn't come back into my life again during this moment such as making music because I no longer felt close to it which still affected me as music has always set me free and it still continues to help me feel like I hadn't ever been abused as times. However, as so much more has happened since I was sixteen years of age, I don't feel completely free from it all.

This motivated me to find a new instrument to start enjoying and at first I started playing the kalimba on my phone, but in the end, I started to enjoy the glockenspiel even more that I had bought as an actual instrument.

I also started to do Art Therapy at home and even though I had bought several art supplies towards the end of 2023, I hadn't fully started enjoying it until talking therapy had begun in February 2024 with the help of my therapist, and around this time, I had also started putting together 3D puzzle models.

Originally, the plan was to create ASMR videos for YouTube, but as my life changed over a few months, so did my plans for YouTube, especially after the distant Reiki Healing towards the end of 2023. No matter how unbearable it was to live with my new reality, I needed to stay focused and not allow my mind to put a plan in place again to end my life, because it would have been very easy to take that step.

There was something that I had wanted to start doing for so long and that was to start playing pool again and also try out snooker at a place close to me, so this was also something that I started doing from mid-April 2024, but it wasn't on a weekly basis. The experience as a whole was both positive and negative because it had been an entire year since I was around complete strangers, so I had pushed myself to the limit of my mental health as social anxiety was still at its highest.

I had played snooker for a whole hour and I was very tired at the end of it, but instead of leaving, I stayed for another hour to play a few games of pool because I wanted to see how I would feel if I pushed myself to stay out longer while also understanding how severe the social anxiety really was? This was because I needed to help myself gain back all of the confidence, energy, self-belief, self-esteem and self-respect that I had lost if I wanted my life to change for the positive because I wasn't going to be able to change my present reality by not challenging myself.

Even though everything that had happened was completely out of my control, changing my life was in my control and there were no excuses, so regardless of how deeply impacted I was, I still had the responsibility of taking the steps that needed to be taken in order for me to finally reclaim my life by knowing that this time, no one would be able to stop me from being the person that I would choose to become!

I had also decided to focus on growing my YouTube channel by posting videos every week, which were mainly YouTube Shorts, as my mental health continued to twist my thoughts. This prevented me from posting videos that involved sharing my life lessons and insights about healing, my perspective on various aspects of mental health, and so on.

My aim was to share the insights and life lessons that I had gained since I was a child by speaking about it with art being involved at times in order for others to be heard and to be seen within their own healing / recovery to then start a new life and as my end goal was to still become an International Public Speaker, posting YouTube videos to start making a name for myself was the beginning of that journey before then putting shows together around the world.

This was the plan anyway and however it would unfold and what I may find myself really doing, I remained open to it, so I didn't make my plans feel like a certainty, as that had always led to disappointments.

Nevertheless, my knowledge of living through and surviving several forms of abuse before being able to start a new life no matter how much loss has occurred is what I am left with, so whatever I will find myself doing in the end, the knowledge will always be shared with the entire world in whatever ways I will find myself sharing it.

The scenario that I remained certain about is that my knowledge will always continue to help others even after my time in this world is over in not only making the right informed choices to address the abuse and the injuries, but they would also be able to understand the journey of starting a new life and how it was possible to still experience happiness after several losses that may have occurred outside of their control because all of the work that I will have produced will always continue to live on.

The one thing that I wanted to destroy from my life completely during this entire detox was using alcohol to cope and get through the week because it had been something that I had done since 2022. Even though it had started as something to help me cry, it slowly turned into something very destructive that had led to a toxic cycle of substance abuse and this was something that I understood in talking therapy during April 2024 because it's where I had gained the clarity to know that I had become an alcoholic.

Sure, I may not have been drinking every single day but using hard spirits each week between 2023 to 2024 to the point where I was completely wasted was more than just casually drinking, especially when I no longer enjoyed it and started to have the worst hangovers.

To admit to myself that I had become an alcoholic was something that I had never even considered before because I didn't see it as that scenario, as I thought I would only be an alcoholic if I was drinking it each day. But when I thought about what was happening in between each drinking session that always felt like a ritual, I craved it and I needed it because without it, I couldn't seem to function.

The thing that almost broke me completely, and it almost led to having a plan to end my life put back in place was to say aloud that the Metropolitan Police Force had turned me into an alcoholic from the severe distress that they had caused when I had worked so hard to never use any alcohol to cope with anything between 2011 to 2021.

It angered me so much that I didn't know how to process this fact because every single officer that had played a role in causing the distress and the officers that stood by their guilty colleagues than admitting I was failed, their life had always continued and wasn't affected in any way while they also allowed the abusers to continue living their lives without it being affected in any way, but mine had slowly been destroyed completely to the point that I was quite literally taken so close to my death on more than one occasion.

I found myself living in the same scenario once again but this time it was against the Metropolitan Police Force where I wanted every single officer that had played a role in causing me distress and staying silent about their colleagues failing me to suffer so much that they understood the pain they had caused me! I found myself wishing that karma hit them so hard that they would never forget what they had done to me!

This was the exact scenario that I found myself living with since February 2016 against all of the abusers after reporting the eldest male sibling and now it was a scenario that I was living with against both the abusers and the Metropolitan Police Force! It was completely unbearable and for anyone that understands this scenario from living through it, you will agree when I say that sometimes, it feels good to fantasize about revenge just to get through the next minute let alone an entire hour, but only to think about it and not actually do it.

How can this much injustice exist where you can have evidence to prove beyond reasonable doubt that a crime has occurred against you and instead of a police force doing what they're supposed to be doing, they leave you feeling like you're a case to be closed and what you have experienced isn't something that needs to be taken seriously?

The way I view officers that don't care about serving people is completely different to how I used to view them and it's quite interesting how my mind has now processed everything in order for me to view the world in the ways that I do today.

Police officers that don't care are simply politicians dressed as police officers, but they will always remain politicians. After all, they are known to be office holders than employees, so my new way of thinking is quite accurate in that sense.

As it got towards mid-May 2024, I found myself experiencing extreme bursts of anger from slowly processing everything further and beginning to let go of what I couldn't change.

This was a continuous experience since the end of 2022 where whenever I would start to let go of another aspect of the past, I would find myself becoming even more affected that made me wonder just how bad things would really become and would it lead to a certain scenario of complete destruction?

I also wondered what my reality would be over the next few months because if I received a reply from the High Court, then I wouldn't be able to start building a new life for a while as I would still be living in the past from the legal battles that would continue.

In the end, I decided to wait until mid-May 2024 and when I still hadn't received a reply; I contacted the High Court to see if a message could be passed onto Dame Victoria Sharp DBE, the President of the King's Bench Division in the High Court, as I had written the letter to her personally.

The person that I had spoken with explained that they couldn't help as they didn't have the contact details for Dame Victoria Sharp DBE or knew what department the letter would be in, so I just needed to wait for a reply? I was left feeling completely alone, and it also felt like it really was the end of the battle that I had fought since I was a child.

Since August 2019, I had to keep putting my life on hold and had found myself continuously waiting for several criminal investigations, complaints and the civil action to be over with that had led to a severe decline within my overall health, so I wasn't prepared to keep waiting around once again to see if I would hear back as my gut instincts kept telling me that the end had finally arrived.

Even though I had accepted that I may never get to experience the justice that I had always deserved, I still wondered if I would hear back and the more I thought about it, the more anger I continued to experience. This is because there isn't a single person in this entire world who can live with this amount of injustice and then just get on with their lives like it's that easy, right?

In the end, I reflected over it all and decided that if I did receive a reply by mid-June 2024 and it stated that my entire case would be heard, then I didn't need to write about it in this book by pushing the publication date back as the case would be heard by the entire world and for that reason, it would be spoken about publicly.

The final thing that I had decided to do to try and start building a new life was to face something that I didn't want to deal with and that was to achieve Functional Skills Level 2 in English and Maths as I hadn't achieved those in high school. I would have gained those qualifications through my apprenticeship in 2021, but life had taken over once again.

Even though I wasn't able to work during this time because of my mental health that remained extremely unpredictable, I had the time to focus on gaining those qualifications, so I didn't have to bother with them later on and cause myself any unnecessary stress.

I just hoped that I finally passed them both on my first try, and with that hope, I wondered where my life would now take me if it really was the end of the battle to addressing the abuse that resulted in complete injustice because of the Metropolitan Police Force treating me like I was nothing more than a case to be closed rather than a human being that was literally screaming out for help!

Chapter Seven

You Will All Burn

For a while, I had been watching videos on YouTube of people explaining what the afterlife is like and many have explained it as a time to rest first when a soul has experienced a very challenging life before having a life review and this is what my reality had become.

After experiencing such a traumatic life, I was now resting as much as I could while trying not to allow my mind to control me any longer because the majority of the thoughts that I had, they all led to either revenge or ending my life. At the same time, I had already started having a life review that was very unsettling.

The emotional and psychological pain that I continued to experience impacted my ability to stay focused within the present because the more I reviewed a life that I had once known, the more broken and helpless I felt. Experiencing all aspects of life was very possible when I escaped in October 2018 and by April 2024, many aspects had been stolen from me without me ever experiencing them; how could life be so cruel?

As I continued to review my life, I found it completely unbearable when I began seeing everything in a completely different way, and it kept me feeling so trapped. This is because those that have harmed me, they were rewarded with a life of freedom and those that failed me;

they were allowed to continue being in a position of power without any real consequences for their actions, but my life was left completely destroyed even when I had done everything that I could to safeguard a life that I desperately wanted to experience.

The further I went into my life review, the more I understood how helpless I had remained since I was a child because in a way, I had always been alone from living through various experiences that others may have never experienced, so only I was able to feel the weight of the pain that I continued to feel.

I think back to when I was seven years of age and choosing to stay in an environment to simply know why the male parent felt they were getting a better brother, so if I wanted to open the front door and leave, then I could? Why didn't I just pick up the phone and call for the police or knock on someone's door and ask for help as I was already in tears?

This is when my entire life could have been different and all of the abuse that I lived through after that day and until this moment, it may have never happened? I have continued to think about this and I have always envisioned what my reality could have been like today because I know that I would have held onto the social worker and begged them to take me from there, but there is also a possibility that my life in a care home may not have been abuse free, so it's a catch twenty-two.

Nevertheless, one of my biggest regrets will always be not calling for help because surely my life wouldn't have been as worse as it has been until now? Maybe I would have been adopted by a family that would have genuinely loved me and maybe I would have lived happily ever after?

Anything would have been better than the life I have lived because there is nothing worse than being born and growing up in an environment where you end up feeling like you're the adopted one that they don't really love but they keep you for the money because that's literally what it felt like from everything that I experienced.

I then think about every other moment when my life could have changed for the better, but the more I reflected over it, the more I realised the only time I would have been okay with not needing to know why someone would treat a child in such a cold-hearted way is when I was seven years of age. This is because after this age, I was brainwashed in such an extreme way that it was impossible to just escape and live my life when there was so much that I remained uncertain about, so I needed answers and a certainty that I wasn't going to be in any danger.

When a person has continuously been telling you that the worst kinds of people want you dead and they will even come after your wife and children unless you have killed them and shown them you're not a coward, that fear becomes your reality and because I remained alone and had no one to help me think logically, I remained brainwashed.

For this reason, when I escaped in October 2018, I was fully prepared because not only did I know the truth, but I also knew who I needed to keep out of my life for good and that's literally what saved me in the end. Anyone that has experienced narcissistic abuse will know that if you remain in contact with someone who is speaking with the people that have hurt you, then you will always find yourself going back to them and being abused all over again.

The time where escaping could have been possible was when I was nineteen years of age, but from how depressed and suicidal I remained, I wasn't in a calm and logical mindset to think about an escape plan because I didn't even know how to travel on the London Underground as looking at the tube map felt so confusing, so to know about renting a place to live in, I would have struggled more than just a little.

No matter how many times or how many ways I will look at the past, I will always come back to the epiphany that I experienced in August 2016 because it's the only one that makes any sense and if it's something that I hypnotised myself to believe in a moment of madness, then so be it because it's the only thing that has continued to keep me going.

However, I then think back to all of the light-bulb moments that I have experienced over the years and from receiving the answers that I have needed to make sense of everything, I know that I have always been watched over and guided by higher powers, so the life that I have lived through might be one that I had chosen because I have always been a healer and through my experiences, including the insights and life lessons that I now have, I am going to continue helping so many more people while empowering change throughout the entire world.

As it got towards the end of May 2024, I found myself feeling conflicted once again because no matter how hard I tried to stay focused on the present moment; I kept finding my thoughts mixed into the chaotic past because by still not being able to cry, the trauma that continued to affect me internally had begun spiraling out of control and I just wondered whether I would actually start living a life that I had never known or would I find myself having to leave this world after all?

It became a very uncertain time once again and this time; I had fully decided that I didn't want any help anymore because if this sort of life was the one that I would continue to experience where I couldn't even work that would help me to build a new life, then I didn't want to try and keep surviving anymore.

What made it feel certain was finding myself looking up pre-paid funeral plans while thinking about the plan that had already been in place because it's the plan that I would still put into action. From being able to see a life for myself after completing therapy, I was left feeling like I didn't have much of a life to look forward to by slowly losing complete interest in everything.

The hobbies and interests that I had started enjoying, I no longer felt the joy because it kept feeling like I was only wasting my time by trying to keep myself distracted from how broken I still truly felt. When I thought that I had experienced the closure that I needed by producing the film, it began feeling like the pain from the injustice would continue rising and hit me when I least expected it.

How can anyone just draw a line under everything that had happened and get on with their life when there was no life that had been experienced in the first place and only teasers of a life that would have been? The more I thought about just how much injustice is involved; the more pain I continued to experience.

I would find myself looking around my flat just as I had been doing a few months prior, and it didn't even hurt anymore to think about breaking and throwing away the 3D puzzle models that I had built for my self-care because all I experienced was complete silence and that silence continued to scream within.

All I had ever wanted since I was sixteen years of age was to live my life, but clearly living a life isn't something that the abusers thought I deserved as they saw me as a house slave and nothing more. They hurt me in the most unimaginable ways and the time I reported everything because there was no other way to let it go after waking up screaming and shouting for several weeks, the Metropolitan Police

Force decided to destroy my entire life and put me through almost five years of complete torture after already failing me in June 2016!

How can anyone just get on with their life after the further distress where complete injustice remains the outcome!? I continued to question whether I should have started legal proceedings, but I knew that being compensated wouldn't be enough because I also wanted several officers to be criminally investigated and prosecuted from the corruption that has taken place!

I already knew that the chances of me getting my desired outcomes were very low, so the only thing that made sense was no longer being in this world because not only would I finally stop hurting, but everything would be addressed because my death wouldn't just be able to be ignored when the way I would leave would allow the entire world to know why I had decided to end my life in the end.

During this time, I thought about the movie Pan's Labyrinth because it felt like I was in Ofelia's shoes quite literally. When Ofelia failed to complete the tasks that she had been set, it meant that she would never be reunited with her family, but she refused to give her brother to be sacrificed because it was more than she could have ever been able to live with. Instead, she sacrifices herself that allows her to be reunited with her family and also completing her journey.

With my life, I refused to take the steps that would have put my youngest brother in a care home where he may have been abused and after knowing what trauma does to a person by experiencing it myself, I couldn't allow myself to do such a thing because I would have never been able to live with such reality, so I sacrificed my freedom in order to make sure that he had a life to live without having to heal through similar traumas as myself.

Even though he had witnessed so much within the toxic environment that the abusers had created, he hadn't directly experienced the type of abuse that I had, so even though he would be processing what he had witnessed, he doesn't have the type of traumas that I will be living with for the rest of my life.

Furthermore, it also felt like my death could lead to the systematic changes that have always been needed and what if my fate was always going to be having to sacrifice myself like Ofelia? What if my journey would also be completed in the same way because no matter how hard I tried to see a life for myself, it felt like within a few months I wouldn't be alive anymore and I was completely okay with that.

As I thought about what my reality could end up being in a few months, I brought myself back to when I was around twelve years of age, as this is when the suicide ideation had begun. I can't remember whether it had started before or after the eldest male sibling had sexually abused me, but it most definitely played a role in feeling completely disconnected from reality as a whole.

While listening to Left Outside Alone by Anastacia on repeat every night, it continued to feel like I was in between earth and the afterlife, which remained my reality even at thirty-two years of age. Even though I have always been made to feel like I don't belong in this world by several people over the years, it truly feels like I don't belong in this world anymore.

Anyone that isn't trauma informed would become concerned if they heard me explain that I have continued to think about ending my life since I was a teenager, but for me, it brings comfort to know that there is a way out if things become more than just unbearable. It's also the scenario that I don't want to end my life because I hate my life, it's simply that so much injustice has happened where the pain has only risen than become completely calm.

We live in a world where those that are causing such harm get to have complete freedom by remaining criminals, but if you have experienced the abuse and you then report it to experience the justice that you deserve within a courtroom, then you will be left even more distressed than you may have already been feeling. How can the world be this unjust and then, when you try and have the support in place, so you can get the help that you need in order to continue living, you find yourself struggling to even survive?

When I think about my entire journey as a whole, I don't think a single day has gone by since I was nineteen years of age where I wasn't struggling through something because one way or another, once the system becomes involved in your life, it becomes almost impossible to no longer be dependent on the system.

If there was one thing that I would have changed that would have allowed me to not remain dependent on the system, then I wouldn't have moved onto Employment and Support Allowance before calling the ambulance on Monday 28th November 2011. The only thing the male parent cared about was using me for money and if finally there was no way for him to get money from me, then maybe my life would have changed for the better?

This is me just remaining hopeful while going through an entire life review, but I don't really know what would have helped me during that time because I needed the truth. As I had no one to help me understand what I realised in 2016 after giving a Video Recorded Interview to the police for the abuse that I had experienced by the eldest male sibling, it was impossible to not remain brainwashed and controlled.

For this reason, even if I hadn't moved onto Employment and Support Allowance, there is a possibility that the male parent would have twisted everything in order to have me claim that social security before taking every penny like he did. There is also a possibility that if I had felt better and had been able to get a job, then the male parent may have taken all of my earnings with the full support of the female parent because without her support, I wouldn't have been abused for several years and in the ways it had happened!

From being uncertain about how I truly felt towards her including the younger male sibling, I was now fully aware because not a single time did they help me and the only times the female parent spoke about how she felt when I almost took my life and again when I was being financially abused is because of the guilt that remained inside of her for not doing and saying anything sooner.

After all, if she truly loved and cared about me as her child, then she would have never spoken to and treated me in the ways that she did since I was only seven years of age! The amount of hate that I have towards those that have abused me and those have failed me is so extreme that if I was to witness them being beaten so brutally, then I wouldn't do anything to help them because they all left me for dead!

One way or another, they will all have to answer for their words and actions that harmed me in the end, so no matter how much freedom they might be experiencing right now, it won't last forever and sooner or later, they won't be able to stop the karma that hits them harder than the truth of how they left me feeling!

As the days went by, I found myself still feeling certain about ending my life and this time it wasn't because I was in any crisis. It was because there was no way to process the amount of injustice that I continued to live with. The more I tried to let go of the past, the more affected I became, and when I thought about the life that I was trying to build, it no longer exited me.

I had lost all joy for life as a whole and the only thing that could have changed that reality was experiencing the justice that I had always deserved that was very possible, but because the Metropolitan Police Force destroyed my entire life and then covered up what really happened on the 24th June 2016, it had turned into the same toxic cycle of how I had felt towards the abusers for several years.

Even though I still felt the same amount of anger towards the abusers, my anger towards the Metropolitan Police Force became so much more as they are the ones that allowed the abusers to keep their freedom while enabling their harm towards me by failing me in every single way possible!

It was bad enough to be told that the evidence wasn't strong enough when several confessions are written all over the pages, but to then put me in a scenario where it felt like it was my word against the officers; they don't care about justice!

Everything started to feel so extreme and the pain within felt like a chemical reaction that could erupt at any second. No matter how hard I tried to keep myself calm, I would experience sudden bursts of anger continuously and to keep my focus on anything in order to try and experience some self-care no longer worked.

Not only had I lost all hope to still experience somewhat of a life after everything that I had lived through, but it also kept feeling like the end was arriving and there was nothing that I could do about it because it felt like my purpose to be in this world had been fulfilled. It kept feeling like I was only born to experience the pain that I had lived through and then sharing the knowledge with the world, so changes could be made within the system and those that lived through similar experiences would become aware on how to better help themselves.

The more I thought about it, the more certain I felt, and even though I was experiencing so much emotional and psychological warfare internally, while remaining uncertain about what my reality could be within a few months, I started to feel a certain calm by knowing that if ending my life is what the outcome would be, then I was ready for it without trying to stop myself this time around.

How much more abuse could a human being experience and then be forced to live with the trauma that was never their own to carry? This question continued to tickle my brain cells while I tried to ignite a new fire within, as the one that had remained lit, it had been killed.

Monday 27th May 2024 had arrived and this very same day in 2016, the female parent had shown me that she had fully taken the side of a narcissistic abuser than care more about the child that had always spoken up for her. I kept wondering how could I have remained so blinded of always being neglected by her, but how could I have known any different when abuse had become so normalised?

I thought back to this day and then the events that followed which angered me so much from being aware that I was never truly in control of my life or my decisions because they were always influenced by the trauma that I continued to find myself living with. When one event would end, it wouldn't take long for another to begin and now I understand it was because both abusers wanted to make sure that they kept me their house slave for the rest of my life.

There are several moments of chaos that I still experience because it doesn't matter how differently I may have lived my life by making different decisions as they wouldn't have helped me when the abusers had always found a way to ruin my plans in order to bring me back into their control once again.

This scenario reminded me of September 2017 when I had planned to become self-employed full-time and finally sign off of social security, but before I could even do this, I found myself realising that unless the repossession order was removed, I would become homeless as the abusers had taken the risk to plan this by going to extreme lengths in order to keep me in their control.

When I wrote the document to explain how their actions had impacted me for them to read, I refused to accept that they had controlled me to pay them the money to remove the repossession order by making me so vulnerable, but in the end, I have to finally be honest with myself; I cared more about my safety than anyone else's.

This is because my youngest brother wasn't my responsibility and it wasn't my job to save him when I didn't put him in that position. I also knew that the council would provide the abusers and my youngest brother with housing as he was only fourteen years of age, so there weren't any problems with them being homeless, but I would have been out on the streets as there was no one to help me!

At the same time, I thought about how his life would be impacted because the place where the council may have provided housing could have been around gangs and I knew that he would suffer so much because of the actions of the abusers! As the months went by, I knew just how desperate they had become to keep me as their house slave and finally, in October 2018 when I couldn't keep hoping that my life would change by living there before escaping, I had no other option but to escape the torture chamber that I had been made to live in.

It doesn't matter how many ways I think about that time and what could have changed everything because the only thing that would have helped was having an income, but I knew that the moment the abusers realised that I was making an income, they would have left me to take on the responsibility that they had always planned to give me without discussing it with me as they had only seen me as a house slave and not their child to love, to care for and to protect!

From November 2011 until October 2018, I did everything to try and put my health first because this was the reason I decided to become self-employed, as I couldn't have the usual retail or admin job. My mental health had always remained impacted and after the 24th June 2016 incident, it wasn't even about living anymore.

The way everything unfolded, I couldn't have done anything differently because I had always done my best at the time, so it doesn't matter how I look at the past because not for a single second was I not surviving. Every single second was pure survival and if I had people that guided me correctly and cared more about my truth than leaving me traumatised further, then things would have turned out differently.

For this reason, I can't regret the decisions that I made when they were all made with my gut instincts because they are the signs and the messages that were being received by higher powers that have always been watching over me. Yes, there were times when I didn't listen to my gut instincts and I paid the ultimate prices for them, but my life couldn't have turned out any differently while I was living in such an abusive environment.

By the end of March 2016, I had achieved the mission that I had been on since November 2011 of wanting to know the truth, and by the end of September 2017; I knew who I needed to keep out of my life for good. Around this same time, I had become comfortable with looking after myself and by the end of September 2018; I knew that my life was no longer going to continue by being around the abusers anymore.

The way everything unfolded since December 2015, I couldn't have changed any aspect of it because every step was a learning lesson and every scenario gave me even more insights into what the truth really was, so there isn't a single thing that would have made life any better because even though I wished the outcomes could have been different, living my life was still possible when I escaped, even though I was left with so much trauma to process, but it hadn't become permanent.

Those that are responsible for enabling the abuse further by leaving me in an environment where I could have been killed and then causing so much more distress to the point that the trauma I was living with had become permanent, they are the Metropolitan Police Force!

Not only did they grant the abusers with complete freedom even though the evidence has confessions written all over it, but they destroyed my entire life in the process and then denied all liability while making me feel like I was just a case to be closed; the entire world will hear about it!

By mid-June 2024, I had requested the majority of the documents that were relevant to the 24th June 2016 incident, between August 2019 to April 2023, and the civil claim because I was now preparing for my future. After reading over the 24th June 2016 documents, I understood what could have happened from the details being fabricated as I was left with two scenarios.

The first scenario came across as being the likely outcome, but there was a specific aspect that made it seem like otherwise. From the report that was recorded on the system where what I had stated wasn't mentioned, the officers may have spoken to the male parent after I was told to go for a walk and the lies that the male parent had stated were then reported on the system only?

The second scenario could be that details from what was stated during the trial of the acts that the female parent had carried out on the 27th May 2016, various details could have been used to cover up the failures that had occurred and if the complaint was so straight forward from what is written within, then why would the complaint take over two years to be investigated? Something just doesn't add up and since the very beginning, I have always felt it!

What doesn't make sense is how the secondary stage officer had stated over the phone something along the lines of 'it seems like you are being emotionally abused', but the male parent was seen as the second victim rather than the suspect when I had given both of their names as the suspects while over the phone when calling for the police, so why wasn't the female parent's name on the report also?

All of the details that don't add up bring it to a conclusion that a cover-up has taken place because from what really happened and what is stated on the complaint outcome report, it makes it seem like a completely different incident has occurred!

The amount of anger that remained present was even more than what I had experienced in the past few months because after reading over the documents and emails again, I had also realised that from what the investigating officer had expressed, he had formed a conclusion from the very beginning by saying that 'a proportionate of the handling of the incident was done correctly and he agreed with it?'

This was by reading the incident report only and not even getting started with the investigation into the complaint, so he remained biased from the very beginning! By agreeing with only a proportion of the crime report, does that mean that the rest of it isn't something he agreed with? I had asked him to explain what he meant, but I didn't even receive a reply?

Everything that I was experiencing emotionally, psychologically and even physically, it gave me the certainty of knowing just how accurate I was when I stepped away from the civil claim and made a life saving decision to destroy all of the documents because I now know for a fact that I would have been found dead after reading over the documents and realising this horrifying truth at that time!

From being able to see things a lot more clearly after stepping away from it all and then coming back to it once I felt emotionally safe, I felt that I needed to bring closure to the 24th June 2016 by doing something more than just releasing a trailer for this book.

I decided to enquire to see if the complaint report for the 24th June 2016 could still be reviewed by explaining my reasons that I felt were very reasonable and after receiving an email to confirm it would be reviewed, I wondered what could be all of the possible outcomes?

Even though I knew not to get my hopes up, I still contemplated what my reality could become if the outcome stated what I have always known to be the truth. Regardless of how the events would unfold and if starting legal proceedings will be the action that I take in the end, then I didn't need to write about it, as I would be speaking publicly. At the same time, I would be trying to build a new life that I could remain happy with while doing whatever I could to keep healing the silence.